T0064496

YOUR CHOICE IN MEN

YOUR CHOICE IN MEN

Why You Seem to Attract the Wrong Ones

CURTIS JORDAN

authorHOUSE®

AuthorHouse™
1663 Liberty Drive
Bloomington, IN 47403
www.authorhouse.com
Phone: 1 (800) 839-8640

Published by AuthorHouse   11/04/2015

ISBN: 978-1-5049-2664-5 (sc)
ISBN: 978-1-5049-2663-8 (e)

Library of Congress Control Number: 2015912402

Print information available on the last page.

Any people depicted in stock imagery provided by Thinkstock are models, and such images are being used for illustrative purposes only. Certain stock imagery © Thinkstock.

This book is printed on acid-free paper.

This book is dedicated to a single event in my life that I have never forgotten and have carried around as a fuel to push me to always do better. When I was around fourteen years old and in high school, there was a particular teacher I really liked, mainly because I had what you could call a schoolboy crush on her. It doesn't take much for a fourteen-year-old boy to have a crush on an adult, but she was just the best teacher in my eyes at the time. Our class was scheduled to do something unique that would change my life forever; she had evaluation sheets that we all had to fill out.

Based on our answers, the sheets would tell us what professions we would be suited for. I was excited to do the profession survey because I was trying to figure out what I wanted to be when I grew up. Throughout school, I had seen firefighters and police officers come to my school to encourage us and show us what an education can do for us. I still wasn't sure if I even wanted to be a part of those professions. Remember: I was fourteen years old, and running into a house fire wasn't my goal at the time; all I would do was run out of a house during a fire.

The results of the evaluations would take a few weeks, so I didn't think much more about my results until they came back. One day when I went to her class, the teacher said, "All right, everyone, I have the results of your evaluations." I was so excited to see what profession I would best be suited to do. I sat patiently while I watched my classmates go up and receive their survey results from the teacher. She looked at each of the student's results first and then asked the person to read them aloud to the class.

As I waited for my turn, I heard the kids read their results, saying that they would best be suited as doctors, lawyers, politicians, and many other professions. When the teacher finally called my name, I was excited and nervous at the same time, and as I walked up to receive my results, I noticed that the teacher looked at my survey results as she had done for everyone else who came up. However, her expression was different for me, in that she read the result and looked at me with a slight smirk on her face.

I eagerly reached my hand out to take my results from her. The teacher handed me the paper and asked me to read it to the class. I looked at the results with excitement, and I felt a nervous ball of anticipation. What I read was that I would be best suited to be a janitor. The entire class broke out in laughter, but what I noticed the most was that the teacher was laughing to the point of being in tears. The result of my evaluation tickled my teacher so much that she needed a tissue to wipe the tears from her eyes, and I never forgot it.

It didn't bother me in a bad way, but it made me realize that an evaluation could not determine my future. I am not saying that being a janitor is a bad profession, unless you don't want to be a janitor. I didn't want to be one, so this started a fire in me that never burned out. I was an impressionable boy who was searching for what he wanted to be when he grew up, and I knew there was more inside of me than just being a janitor.

This book has been a lifelong dream that has come true for me. I can't express the joy inside of me to be able to finally express this in a way that I hope helps even just one woman, meaning that I will have accomplished what God gave me.

I dedicate this book to the people who gave me silent confidence at an early age. The love I received growing up as a boy is something that I wish everyone could experience. My parents are Carnel Jordan and Vivian Johnson, whom I have truly gotten to know on a more intimate level as I've grown to become a man. I truly do love the both of you and owe everything to you.

My grandparents, Junious and Mary Porter, raised me as their own and instilled calmness in my character that gave me a base for success. My father figure during my early years as a teenager was my stepfather, Ronald Johnson, who was a great male role model when I needed one. They all made me feel that I could do anything, despite the disorganization of our family tree. This book is proof that what you gave me slowly manifested itself into a belief on my part.

This book has allowed me to appreciate that I always had more inside of me than just being a janitor. I dedicate this book to that fourteen-year-old boy that stood in front of his class reading a sheet of paper that said all I would ever be was a janitor.

My hope is that those who read this book understand that no evaluation, test, or person can direct what God has placed inside of you.

Contents

Chapter 1   What Gives Me the Right?........................... 1

Chapter 2   Attraction 11

Chapter 3   Common Sense... 27

Chapter 4   A Simple Philosophy 37

Chapter 5   I Was the Wrong Man 48

Chapter 6   His Nature... 56

Chapter 7   A Woman in Control................................. 66

Chapter 8   Blaming Yourself Won't Be Easy............... 72

Chapter 9   Change Yourself, Not Him 81

Chapter 10   The Race Card..91

Chapter 11   The Dangers of Compromise 98

Chapter 12   A Good Man is Not Hard to Find 105

Chapter 13   How Many Girlfriends Do You Have?..... 115

Chapter 14   The Word Wrong is a Metaphor.............. 118

Acknowledgments 125

About the Author 127

CHAPTER I

WHAT GIVES ME THE RIGHT?

What gives me the right to write a book concerning the choices women make when it comes to men and relationships? I pose this question because it was the first one I heard when some of my female friends previewed the concept for this book. The question is valid, as you typically do not find a book like this from the male perspective. I took some time to truly understand the question and to come up with an answer.

Men have insight into why a woman may choose a man who is wrong for her. A man can be very slick in the beginning, so a woman may think she's choosing him for the right reasons. But another man will clearly see that he is wrong for her.

I have been married three times—but to only two women. The simple explanation is that I married my high school sweetheart, and then I married the woman I met during our divorce. I married my second wife twice. Although I have always heard advice not to do that, I did it anyway. I loved my second wife very much and felt we would be together forever. But forever is a long time. I was damaged emotionally and didn't know that if I would only be patient, I would save myself a lot of unnecessary pain. Let me explain.

Before the document was drawn up to divorce my first wife, I was developing feelings for the woman who would eventually be my second wife. This scenario happens all the time but is seldom admitted by those in it. I was involved in this weird scenario because I was immature, impatient, and doing what so many women do when they are in love—compromising, making excuses, and accepting a lot of crap—because I thought I couldn't live without her. Truth be told, women, you can and will live without him, and being alone until you find the right person is not a bad idea. But I was in such a rush to be in love that I forgot the basics. I needed to end my current relationship, heal, and learn from it before I started another relationship. So I took a good look at my life, who became the inspiration for writing this book.

I want to start by saying that I dearly loved the women I married and still respect them as the mothers of my children. Looking back, I acknowledge that we were all messed up, and I was chief among them. I am not perfect and realize that most authors of books like this try to present themselves as such. However, my intent is to be informative on this topic and to present something for you to consider—or ignore, if you so choose. The key is that it is *your* choice. But remember: with every choice there are consequences. You must exercise patience for your decision to prove it as a correct one or not.

The best part about making a relationship mistake is that you have the opportunity to learn more about your own flaws and what you need from a man. As you get older, you should start to realize that if you aren't inviting what you need into your life, you will get what you don't want instead.

I needed to be patient when it came to the women I loved and married. Although I was very much in love with them, I was unable to make them stay when they desired something or someone else. I had to come to the understanding that maybe I was the wrong man for them and that they were the wrong women for me at the time. Realizing that you might be the wrong person in a relationship is never easy, but that realization will help you become a better person down the road.

I finally decided to be patient and wait for a woman who would be willing to support me in a way that I needed. I am not going to say that your journey will be easy, but it is necessary for your growth. It was extremely hard for me, because I was so bitter at women and upset with myself for my contribution to the demise of my marriages.

It takes time to truly understand what you need in your life, and time equates to being patient. It takes time to forgive yourself for the wrong you have done, whatever that may have been. I could have lost my mind and acted like a fool, but maybe I wasn't the man for them. If that was the case, I couldn't allow that to stop me from believing that there was someone out there for me if I used better common sense. It all comes down to your decisions and approach when you are *not* getting what you want in a relationship.

Men have similar pressures when it comes to relationships, and those pressures often lead to them making the wrong decisions. I had the same conversations with myself that women have with themselves. Men, like women, battle low self-esteem. We wonder why we aren't good enough for a particular woman and if we will ever find a good woman. You may not know this, though, because men often do not feel safe enough to share these thoughts with anyone.

Decision-making is not gender biased, which means that no man or woman is above making the wrong decision. In regard to your choice in men, a man may be able to recognize why you seem to be attracted to the wrong ones. You must understand that your decision concerning a man has the ability to harm you emotionally, physically, and psychologically. Choosing the wrong man can even cause you to doubt your ability to recognize a good man.

Relationships and marriages are crumbling now more than ever before, but please note that there is nothing wrong with loving people. There is nothing wrong with relationships; rather, flawed people make relationships difficult. There is nothing wrong with the institution of marriage; rather, flawed people make marriage difficult. Flawed people can be selfish within a relationship. When you understand that your selfish desires have nothing to do with what the man is doing or not doing, you will then realize your role in your own unhappiness.

Let me share a story that will explain why I wrote this book about women choosing the wrong men. When I was in the military, there was a woman whom I will call Jane. Jane worked at a satellite hospital that was adjacent to the well-known mother hospital in that area. She was single and looking for love but, unfortunately, in the wrong place.

One weekend Jane met a fantastic guy whom I will call John. She told me that he might be the One. He was fine, well groomed, could sing, and seemed very sweet. Because dating had been difficult for Jane, it was a joy hearing about a man who seemed to have great potential. However, his reputation preceded him, as I knew about his womanizing. When Jane asked for my opinion concerning him, I couldn't tell her what she wanted to hear. I could only tell her the truth.

I wasn't sure why she even wanted my opinion, and then I realized that she was desperate. I advised her to leave John alone because he was no good when it came to relationships. I explained that he would dog her out in several different ways and that he may spend her money, eat all her food, and run up the mileage on her car. This information killed some of her excitement, but it was what she needed to hear. I understood her disappointment, but she had to hear the truth from someone who was not emotionally attached to the situation or the outcome.

Still, Jane began dating John anyway, who slowly started doing exactly what I said he would. He started spending her money, as he had access to her checking account, drove her car while she was at work, stole money from her, and ate her food. He even stole one of her credit cards.

This relationship messed Jane up for a long time, and it all came back to her decision to ignore my advice. She made a decision that I would presume was out of loneliness and the illusion of what she thought was her dream man, which soon turned into a complete nightmare.

I just could not understand why she asked me about John if she wasn't going to listen, but then it dawned on me. She had to date him until she understood that her problems with men had nothing to do with them. Unfortunately, they had everything to do with her decisions when choosing them.

The point I'm making is that in our attempts at finding love, we oftentimes ignore what we see; sometimes we also ignore good, sound advice from others who have our best interests at heart. Love is a powerful thing, and it should never be underestimated, because it is something that we all crave and need as human beings. So in attempting to answer the question "What gives me the right to tell a woman anything about men and relationships?" I actually don't feel that I have the right to tell a woman anything, but I have the responsibility to speak out about a situation that could damage her emotionally. It doesn't matter who the woman happens to be. We all should look out for one another whenever possible, and that concept has been lost in our selfish society.

The truth is that some women may be the cause of their own emotional pain and may not even realize it. Decisions are important, so we need to make every decision with great care, for we sometimes have no idea of its consequences until the damage has been done to our self-worth. We make decisions on who to date, who to have sex with, who to marry, and when to have kids, so how can we continue to go through life thinking our decisions are meaningless? A bad decision can impact our lives dramatically. A decision can be life or death even under the most innocent of circumstances.

I have spoken with women who said they married without even loving the person that they married. Who does that? I will tell you who does that: a person who had the wrong intentions and a woman who was broken and never allowed herself to heal, which led to that terrible decision. Instead of healing, she continued the cycle in a broken state of consciousness and never really experienced true love in the end. When a woman is broken, she will normally use her bad experiences as a warning to the younger generation regarding what not to do in a relationship. The bad experiences serve as a guide, but oftentimes it is misguided to the very person delivering the message. You will hear a person say, "Watch out for this type of guy," and "Watch out when he says this to you," and "Don't ever let a man do that." Decisions are what created those bad experiences. Because she can blame the guy, she sometimes never blames the decision to be with the guy, even when she knew it was a mistake from the beginning.

I once dated a woman who was instructing her daughter only to date white men. When I came to the house for the first time to be introduced to the family, there was a subtle uproar from her daughter because I wasn't a white man. I heard the daughter talking to her mother upstairs, saying, "All this time you've been telling me to date this way, and you bring something else home." This was a poignant moment for me, for I became "something else"—and I stopped being a man who wanted to love her mother.

Truth be told, I made a bad decision that day myself, for this woman told me that she was not looking to date a guy like me but I seemed to be different. I knew I had become a science-fair project, but I stayed anyway, like a dummy. I knew going in that this would be difficult, but I still did it and suffered some emotional hurt because of my inability to recognize that my decision was a bad one in that moment. Let's just say that it was the longest year and a half of my dating life. I would have been perfect for her if I were white, but my color and her experience with black men in the past got in the way of her belief that a black man could never do right by her and that he would always let her down. I chose to speak on this topic because I have seen it, lived it, and am also a product of bad decisions over the years.

I care about people in general, and if I can expose something or say something that might minimize the possibility of a hurtful situation, I will attempt to do so. Decisions come with consequences and can be extremely costly, depending on how bad the decisions are as well as the circumstances surrounding them.

As for Jane, she will ultimately be fine physically, but the emotional cost may be felt down the road when she meets a nice guy who is confused by how she is treating him. He will have no idea that John was able to damage Jane emotionally concerning men years earlier. I did not have the ability to control Jane's decision, but I attempted to inform her about something that I knew more about than she did.

If you knew the ramifications of your decisions at the beginning, before they were carried out, I wonder if you would make the same decisions. If you knew that a decision that makes you feel good now would mess you up—and perhaps your children—later, would you still make that decision? If you knew the decision to date that man now would cause you to have trust issues later, would you still date him? I gather you answered those questions appropriately by saying no. But a lot of us, including myself, often ignore the warnings and our own instincts because somehow we think it can't happen to us. The decisions made today will determine your future as far as relationships, self-esteem, and how others view you.

I will continue to sound the alarm if I notice that the pathology of a decision in choosing a man might be the reason for unnecessary hurt. There are times when a man has the ability to pour kindness into a woman's life, and although it may be totally unexpected and can oftentimes be rejected, that won't stop me from trying. If God is able to speak words of wisdom through a donkey, then I would hope that what I have is a simple concept that could help someone. The ability to make the right decisions is not gender based. We all make bad decisions when it comes to relationships, but I hope you allow me to share something that you may not have thought about and may want to consider.

CHAPTER 2

ATTRACTION

Attraction is a peculiar thing that can be hard to explain, and it's difficult to put your finger on the reason it is so powerful. When choosing the right man, it is oftentimes an art in which you will find yourself losing more than you win. But losing is not always a bad thing, for growth and learning happen through mistakes. The reason I say that is because we are all attracted to different things at different times in our lives. What I find attractive is not necessarily indicative of what you would find attractive. Attraction is based on individual preferences that are typically born from our experiences and interactions with many people, places, and things during a lifetime.

You may not have been attracted to other nationalities when you were young, but now that you are more mature and your exposure to other people has increased, you may find yourself attracted to other nationalities. The nationality didn't change; you actually changed your view of what is attractive and included such people on your list. If you are currently in a relationship, there was something about that person that attracted them to you. Attraction can be so intense that it pulls you blindly, without you totally understanding the cause of the pull. Different things attract different people in different ways, but we could probably agree that we have all felt an attraction to various people at different times of our lives.

Attraction incorporates the traditional five senses of sight, touch, taste, smell, and hearing. We use these five senses every day, but we are never more aware of it than when it comes to the attraction of the opposite sex. As a woman, have you ever walked past a guy and the subtle aroma of his cologne was so alluring that you just had to give him a compliment about how good he smells? It probably made you do a double take in order to get a second sniff or look at this guy because the smell as he walked by you was attractive. The corresponding actions, comments, and compliments are all tangible things we do once our senses have been aroused. These are all the by-products of attraction.

If you are completely honest with me, you have probably had this moment happen to you at one point in your life. While minding your own business, all of a sudden you encounter the most attractive, handsome, and alluring man that you have ever seen in your life. You proceed to express your visual pleasure with a mumbled comment to yourself. If this has happened to you, did you try to take him all in with your eyes? Pupils dilated, head in a steady position, and total attention on the target … We all have an internal image of what we deem attractive to us individually, and when we actually see it, it can be overwhelming in that moment. Where does your image of that perfect person originate from? Think about it …

I remember talking to a certain girl on the telephone for the first time when I was about fifteen. She was around the same age, but she went to a different school. I remember being nervous to call her on the telephone and speak with her for the first time. You see, she was a blind date setup from a friend of mine, so I was blind to what to say or how to respond on the phone. I got up the nerve to call her and immediately developed knots in my throat as I picked the phone up and dialed the number. Once it started to ring, talk about scared—I was a nervous wreck. A woman answered the phone.

I responded nervously, "Hi, may I please speak to Jocelyn?" The woman on the other end said, "This is Jocelyn." I was a little confused for a split second because the woman on the phone did not sound like a fifteen-year-old. The voice was full, deep, and entirely mature in tone for her age. I pictured a beautiful woman with jet-black shoulder-length hair and Indian dark-skinned complexion with a dimple. Now, I am not sure how her voice made me imagine all of this, but indeed it did. It left a lasting impression on me to this day. I have yet to hear a voice as attractive as that, which is saying a lot. Her voice alone made me want to meet and get to know her instantaneously. I felt as if I had hit the jackpot.

That's attraction! Of course, in meeting her, she looked nothing as I had envisioned. She wore braces, had a perm that went horribly wrong, and wore big glasses. I'm not proud of my initial response to meeting her, but I was young; I hope I didn't hurt her feelings back then. By the way, she turned out to be the very woman I had envisioned. She was just in the process of her blossoming phase. The duckling phase can be misleading for a guy who is in his superficial phase. In describing this entire scenario, please do not miss the fact that I am talking about internal images of attraction and where they originate. I ask that you do not focus on the fact that I was a jerk at fifteen and my response to Jocelyn was superficial.

Conversations about relationships between men and women can be so controversial that you'd think you were talking about politics or religion. No one is actually listening to the other, but both genders want to be heard. There are so many dynamics about the two genders when it comes to relationships that it would be almost impossible to write a short book. It reminds me of those religious and political arguments that can go on for days with no resolution. There will always be so much passion, so much controversy, and no real answers with topics of this nature. These are never-ending subjects with a myriad of views that can be skewed and biased depending on which religious leader or political representative you ask. It is almost impossible to come to a singular conclusion one way or the other, but there are ways to find some valid commonsense truths that both genders can adopt.

The ability to look into the mirror and take responsibility for choices made is definitely a maturity trait seldom practiced by men and women, especially when it comes to a relationship choice. When it comes to relationships, a woman should always try to make sound decisions based on the facts, because emotions can be very misleading. This may sound easy, as simple as using common sense, but this can be a difficult thing to separate, especially in women, who are designed around emotions. Men tend to leave their emotions in their childhood, so they come into a relationship with a different mind-set than most women. You will have many opportunities to blame a man for so many things down the road that you will lose count, but for now let's talk about choices from a woman's point of view.

I already know that in my research for this book, I will probably be highly criticized for its contents. I'm not sure that I will be criticized for the content as much as I will be criticized because I am a guy writing about something that pertains to women and their decisions in the beginning stages of relationships. I would ask that you allow me to explain another motive for writing such a book geared toward women in the first place. Then maybe you will be able to understand why I felt the need to take on such a dangerous task considering the criticism that may follow.

You may or may not be familiar with the children's movie *Toy Story*, but it serves the purpose in my explanation. If you have never seen the original movie, I would suggest that you take the time to watch it for your own understanding. It's a rather funny animated movie, and I thought of this concept while driving in my car one day. Please don't ask me why I was thinking about a children's movie while driving to work, because I have no idea. I call this analogy "Woody versus Buzz Lightyear."

In today's society, where it is becoming harder and harder for men to understand what women want, mainly because we have neglected to really listen to women in the same way we do our sports analysts, I thought I could relay it in a different way, basing it on these two cartoon characters. You see, *Toy Story* is about the life of a small boy who is growing up. It's about his evolution as a boy and his growing interest in toys. He is a typical boy—rough and rugged. He develops an attraction to a particular toy that was popular during that time in his life. It's a doll in the likeness of a cowboy, and his name is Woody. The toy is a cowboy made from regular cloth with stuffing inside of it. He has a cowboy hat, boots with spurs, and a cowboy belt with a holster for a small toy gun. The Woody doll has a pull cord in his back, and once you pull it, it will say such things as "There's a snake in my boot," "Reach for the sky," and "Somebody poisoned the water hole."

The boy adored that doll and did everything with it; you could say he loved it. The doll was simple—no bells or whistles, low maintenance, didn't need batteries, and was reliable and dependable. As the boy became older, the toy industry started to evolve. A new breed of toy was introduced to the market. This toy had retractable wings, a helmet visor that opened, laser lights, laser sounds, and batteries. The toy was called Buzz Lightyear, and this toy had everything necessary to draw the attention of the boy, as it appeared to be a better doll. The toy even said with a persuasive voice, "To infinity and beyond."

As you can imagine, when the Buzz Lightyear toy came out, it was with great fanfare and advertisement. The boy received one as a gift from his mother and never looked back. He played day and night with Buzz and even slept with him. He forgot about Woody because Woody was now old and Buzz was new and had those bells and whistles that Woody didn't have in his day.

What happens when Buzz Lightyear's batteries go dead and he can no longer produce the sounds and effects that made him appealing? He can no longer speak the words "To infinity and beyond." He no longer has the laser sound or laser light show that drew children to him in the first place.

My middle son still has a Woody doll to this day; we don't exactly know what happened to Buzz Lightyear.

In case you missed it, I want you to remember something important about this movie and my analogy. Please notice that as the boy grew up, Woody never stopped being who he was designed to be and never stopped loving the boy. It was the boy who changed and stopped loving Woody.

Allow me to return to the subject of my motivation behind this book. I had a conversation with a person who is close to me, and she spoke about her relationship when she was young and how it went wrong. I made a mental note during her explanation of things that went wrong in the relationship and decided to write a few things down that night. First and foremost, men come in all shapes, sizes, colors, occupations, and temperaments. Sometimes we can view people in two categories, those you consider to be plain or boring (Woody) and those who have all the bells and whistles (Buzz Lightyear). My point is that sometimes in chasing what society says is the man for you (Buzz Lightyear), you actually overlook your Woody.

So these are my questions: What happens when a woman has made a bad decision in relation to a guy? Is it politically correct for a man to tell her? I would be questioning her decision, which can be seen as an indictment against her intellect, so it would have to be done carefully. I ask that you read this with an open mind and just consider what you are about to read. You may be able to relate to my personal view.

If you can't, then you surely at least know of someone who time after time has developed a relationship with someone who turned out to be the wrong man. The person probably would have not gone through this because it was the wrong man but because she made the wrong decision.

This is the question that I heard the most while writing and sharing an early copy of this book with women: "What gives you the right to tell a woman anything about relationships?" That is an honest question and one that I initially had some trouble answering. The more I thought about why this topic was so important, the more I thought about what triggered me to write this book in the first place. I stated earlier that I had a conversation with someone close to me concerning something she and her boyfriend at the time were going through. I felt that her decision may have contributed to the reason she was unhappy with her situation. I never told her what I was thinking back then, but it became the seed to what has transpired into this book.

I have a genuine concern that bad decisions, whether male or female, expose us all to unnecessary hurts and situations that could have been avoided. That being said, I would hope that my being a man wouldn't interfere with a woman receiving a different view. I just ask that you consider what I am saying, even if deep down you may want to go against what I am saying just because I am a man.

I'm around many women in my field of work, and sometimes I hear them say that they blame men for the reason they are still single. I agree that many men have not taken the responsibility necessary for a healthy relationship, like being a strong friend, boyfriend, husband, father, lover, and protector within the household, as men should be. Some men, including myself, have definitely dropped the baton in several areas. So when I hear some women say that they are single because there is not a good supply of quality men, I don't believe that's true. When you blame men, that excuse can be a crutch that will hide the real reason some women find themselves unable to find the right guy.

The belief is that most good men are gay, married, or on the down-low. However, I can't totally disagree with some of these beliefs. The beliefs may have a grain of truth to them, but they aren't necessarily true. This is not the main reason that a healthy, attractive, and vivacious woman is still single and unable to attract the right guy. Wanting to accept and believe those excuses creates a false sense of blame rather than promotes personal responsibility.

I want to be clear about my next statement: most women have never had a problem attracting men. You may want to disagree with me, but the average woman has never had that type of problem. The problem is more in deciding to pass on a man that she's not meant to be with rather than going with what feels good. There are men out there who love big women, skinny women, tall women, short women, pretty women, ugly women, blondes, redheads, brunettes, bald-headed women, and small people; there are also men who love dead women … so there is no excuse! Attracting is not the problem, nor are men the problem. It boils down to waiting for the *right* man instead of settling for the *right now* man. A woman's lack of patience is the problem, which leads to making a bad decision in choosing the man she needs.

I have often heard that men are intimidated by a woman's education, professional background, or success. If you listen closely, you may also hear yourself reacting the same way toward a man. That is one of the most arrogant and insensitive statements to make as a woman toward the very man you say you want to love and you want to love you. Have you ever considered this option: could it be that he has been taught all of his life to be the provider for his family and now that you indicate in subtle ways that you don't need him or his money, he has nowhere to place himself into your life as a man? It's not that he is intimidated; it's that his definition of a man has been taken away and internally he tries to process everything he has been taught a man is supposed to be by the very society that he is trying to please. He now asks himself an internal question: *So what is my role as a man now if I am supposed to be so intimidated by my woman?*

I ask that you just consider this option rather than the insensitive option: that he is just intimidated by your success. For some men, there may be an element of truth to the intimidation factor, just as there are a percentage of gold diggers who chase men for their money. My point is never to classify all men into a miniscule position unless you want to be classified as well. The average man wants a woman who is successful. What he doesn't want is a woman who uses her success as a poking stick. He has to feel like a man, just as you have to feel like a woman, so don't break your man down, for you both will lose. A degree, PhD, or your success in the business world is a great thing to accomplish in life, but have you had difficulty maintaining a fruitful and fulfilling relationship? It would be foolish to think that any of these reasons are a valid reason as to why you are still single. Listening to the masses will place you in a comfortable environment that surrounds you with women who think just like you and have the same problems with men. The problem is that you can cause yourself to lose reality in a situation when you're trying to relate to others.

These are the things you may talk with each other as women, but if you ask a man if your education, professional success, or the many letters behind your name intimidates him, you'd be surprised with the answer. I want to examine a thought that is not spoken about. Could the reason that some women are still single and attracting the wrong men in their lives have more to do with them and less to do with men?

I say that very carefully because I want you to explore the possibility that sometimes you can create your own lousy relationships with someone you should have never been with in the first place. I will admit that I do not have name recognition going for me, but I have always recognized when I was in a lousy relationship due to my bad decision. I have been single, a teenage parent, married, divorced, cheated on, cheated with, and the other guy in a relationship. I have seen relationships from several different interesting angles from a male point of view, and sometimes experience is the best teacher.

I find myself blessed and privileged to have been around some of the smartest and most innovative, sophisticated, and dumbest men that I have met in my entire life. God has a way of exposing you to not only the smartest minds in the world but also the character-flawed minds as well. I believe that in order to be well rounded, you must meet everyone around the well. There are many people sitting at the well, and you must experience all of them at their levels to understand different points of view. I want to start by saying that the men who have contributed to my life have been great husbands, great fathers, successful entrepreneurs, great friends, and acquaintances to me over the years. In saying that, I was privy to personal information via conversation or observation. A man speaking comfortably around other men is a commodity that the average woman never gets the chance to experience. While a few men were secret sex addicts, overt booty chasers, undercover abusers, obvious deadbeat dads, and licensed womanizers, the majority of my exposure was with real men who loved their women with all of their hearts.

I want to add that I would never consider anyone who abuses his woman physically or emotionally a great man or husband. I do know that where a man lacks in one area, he normally achieves in other areas. For example, I know of a woman who stated repeatedly that her husband was lousy at being a husband but was a great provider.

There is much to learn about people that doesn't always involve the successful sides of their beings. You can be a failure in one area of your life and flourish in another area simultaneously. If you think about it hard enough, you will probably realize that you fall into that category right now. That being said, you would not recognize any of these men with all of their flaws if I were to introduce them to you. These men are regular guys who work hard and tend to play hard, but sometimes their relationships can get lost in the process. They love women just as much as they love what they do professionally.

I believe that in order for a man to be a good husband, he has to see what a good husband looks like from someone who is a good husband, although he may have started out as a lousy one. Then he has to decide to be that good husband that he was meant to be all along. In order for a man to know how to treat women, he has to see a woman being treated well. Then he has to decide to treat his woman well. You can't force a man to do something he is not ready to do or is currently incapable of doing.

That notion goes for women as well, but all too often, we find that we as adults are breeding little players and pimps at an early age. For example, you may have heard this said to a little boy: "He is a cutie; he will be a heartbreaker when he grows up." Words have influence, and they can bring about something in a person that you never expected. That phrase may sound innocent, but to the woman on the other side of that comment, it will not be as innocent as it appears to be right now. On the other side of that phrase is an adult woman looking for love who will soon find heartbreak from this cutie-pie little player who is now a man. That woman could easily be you—or has it already been you?

I am a retired military soldier, so I have seen and experienced a lot of stuff within the military in a short period. The military is a close group of men and women who volunteer to serve our country freely and defend our constitution and our way of living with their lives. Growing up around these professionals that protect our country, you will be exposed to some interesting things. I could share some eye-opening stories, to say the least, but I wouldn't have traded it for the world. Sometimes exposure to things is what you need in order for you to know what to do and what not to do. I have spent time with single men while I was married. I have spent significant time around married men while I was single and divorced. I just hope that my commonsense approach will stop you from worrying about how men think and make you focus on how you maintain core values and standards.

The military exists because of a commonsense approach. They adopted core values and standards in the military when dealing with so many people. How is it that you can bring people from all walks of life, different religions, and all races for one common goal like the military? A core group of values and standards set the tone for what is acceptable and not acceptable. The military doesn't emphasize each individual's differences; they instead focus on what each person has in common with the group, which is to defend. The truth is that not everyone who joins the military comes from a place with values and standards of conduct. The military has to instill that into everyone in order not to miss anyone, for they can't afford to have unruly disorder in the ranks. You will always have some that stray despite the standards set, but everyone knows the standards of conduct.

Do the men in your life know your values and standards of conduct? Do you adjust your values and standards based on the person, your surroundings, or your emotional state? If no one knows your standards, you don't have any standards. If you keep moving the line in the sand on your standards, you don't really have any standards. You will continue to get what you have been getting: the wrong men in your life.

CHAPTER 3

COMMON SENSE

How do you measure the smartness of a person? Some may assume that a person who attends an Ivy League school is smarter than someone who attends a state university. In my opinion, smartness is not a measurable item, because what would be the benchmark for measuring? Some people are good at taking tests, and some are not. I do believe that actions can be a great indicator to measure someone's maturity. I believe that maturity and smarts are closely related, so I will replace smarts with the word maturity.

America is recognized as a country that places special value on someone with the ability to attend the finest schools. A student can receive a scholarship based on his achievements in academics, sports, or other special skills. Einstein was a person of great intelligence and scientific maturity, but was he any smarter than the average person just because he was a scientist? A person of Einstein's caliber would be called smart. He is called smart because he demonstrated a level of maturity in his field that far exceeded the average person. His actions created the pathway for him to be considered smarter than his peers.

We base our entire level of learning on a point scale that leads to a grade denoted by an alphabet of A, B, C, D, or F. There are times when society may judge your personal level of intelligence based on how many letters follow your name, your accomplishments, how much college you have under your belt, how you look or what you don't have as compared to others. If you are a person with a degree or several degrees, even though people may not verbalize it, you are esteemed in a high regard amongst the upper echelon of our society. The terms master's and PhD carry a lot of weight that will garnish you respect among your peers as well as in modern-day society.

Sometimes as a self-proclaimed sophisticated society, we fail to realize that other forms of intelligence have nothing to do with professional schooling. They can come naturally or through everyday experiences, but you may never be graded on how well you perform.

In the context of a relationship, there are people who seem to be able to maintain long relationships, while others struggle and have many short-lived relationships. Maintaining a relationship takes a level of maturity that most will never understand. In order to have a fruitful relationship, you have to have the intelligence to understand why you are in a relationship in the first place.

For example, *emotional intelligence* has various meanings, but concerning this topic, I believe that people who possess this are able to adapt to any situation and any people they encounter on a daily basis. They have the ability to detect and decipher emotions in faces, pictures, voices, and even their own emotional changes. They understand themselves and relate well with people. They may not have degrees in this field, but it is clear that they harness an intelligence that few people possess or are able to understand. In other words, this is something that comes natural to them.

People who have *creative intelligence* believe that there is always an answer, or perhaps different answers, that no one has thought of yet. Creative intelligence is looking for answers that haven't been found previously. Not everyone is able to produce this type of creativity, although for some people, this is second nature.

People who have *verbal intelligence* are strong in verbal-linguistic intelligence. These people are able to use words well, both when writing and speaking. These individuals are typically good at writing stories, remembering written and spoken information, and reading. They also enjoy writing and debating or giving persuasive speeches. These people can be teachers, writers, lawyers, or just your neighbor with no formal education. This form of intelligence comes naturally to some people.

Finally, there are the people that I want to focus on in this book. The success of these people is derived from developing the innate ability through everyday learning and putting it to effective practical use. This can be termed as *practical intelligence* or *practical maturity*. Have you ever noticed that there are instances when people who work hard and excel in academics seem to struggle to find success in their careers? There are legendary instances of people who are high school dropouts but still reach iconic status in ventures. You may be experiencing a form of success in your life, whether it is on the job or in business, but find yourself a failure in relationships. This is the time to learn how to adapt to, shape, and conform to your everyday environments. This is the time for the street smart common sense.

The term "common sense" is used when describing the simplest form of making sense. Sometimes we take for granted that everyone has this basic form of sense. In reality, we need to understand that common sense is not so common. I realize that a person's upbringing, experience, and associations can alter the basic logic of what a person can perceive as logical thinking. There is more *un*common sense going on far more than there is common sense. I'm not saying that you don't have common sense, but if you have felt as if you don't make the best choices when it comes to men, then I'm here to tell you that there is a reason behind it.

I often wonder how people with infinite access to information, understanding, and problem-solving tools at their disposal find it hard to use the God-given ability of common sense. I considered some of the decisions I have made during my life versus some of the advice that I have given, and I quickly realized how common it is to have no common sense at all. For example, I knew that having unprotected sex was wrong, but I still did it, for I trusted the woman I was with at the time. Nevertheless, we still had a child early in our teens. I blame myself and no one else. I was told the hazards, but I took the chance anyway. I also cut two fingers off almost completely while playing with a handsaw, even though I was told the hazards of doing so. I found a disparaging difference between my mind-set toward the advice I give versus my mind-set of the advice I receive.

The advice that a person gives is completely based on the facts of a situation. The advice that a person receives is based on the same facts, but here is where you will see the difference. When there is an emotional attachment to the facts, hearing and following advice becomes a harder task than you can imagine. The emotional attachment to the facts creates an evolving sensitivity to the advice that is normally not well received in most cases.

Just remember that advice can oftentimes be misleading. For example, if I tell you that someone did me wrong and I explain how this person did me wrong, I may then ask for your advice and input. Unknowingly, I would anticipate hearing you agree with my version of the situation. We do this all the time but seldom realize it. Now, if you tell me something that goes against what I expected you to say, my first problem with you will be facts and my second problem will be with your advice. Why? The reason is that when I tell you that someone did me wrong, I actually want you to agree that I was done wrong. That is the only reason I told you in the first place. The problem with being told that you were not done wrong but that you may be the guilty party is that your ego may not allow you to admit it. Realistically, no person wants to admit when they are wrong, for that opens us up to being vulnerable or feeling a sense of incompetence depending on the situation. In every argument I have been involved in, I was right every time … If you let me tell it. Frankly what people do you know who want to admit when they are wrong, especially when it means embarrassment?

Here is an example of what I mean … I had a female friend—we will again call her Jane—who was single and preparing to attend training in California. The problem was that Jane was scheduled for a required procedure in Virginia days before she was to attend this training. She was excited to go to California and attend the training as well as go to Disneyland. She would be in the hospital for three days, and she needed help. Her girlfriend—we will call her Sara—heard that she was scheduled for surgery and decided to fly down to help her friend through this time. This was an awesome gesture by Sara, but Jane never expressed her plans to attend the training in California, despite the surgery.

Here is where it got tricky. When Jane had the surgery, she enjoyed the pampering of Sara while she healed in the hospital. Sara took care of her home and sat with her during her stay in the hospital. Once Jane was discharged on day three, instead of going home to rest and cancelling the trip as her doctor suggested, she told Sara that she wasn't going home but instead heading to the airport to attend training in California.

She left Sara in Virginia, who came down expecting to stay for two weeks to nurse her friend back to health. The problem was that Sara wasn't aware of Jane's plans, which left Sara confused. Sara would now have to stay in Virginia until her departure date or pay to have it moved up. She chose to pay and leave Virginia. Jane's statement to me was, "I didn't ask her to come down here to help me, plus I had planned this training trip for months, so I am going to California!"

Jane left on the third day for California, did the training, and went to Disneyland. She had a great trip. When she returned home, she called Sara, wanting to tell her about her trip, but she could not reach her via telephone, cell phone, or e-mail. Jane called me and told me that she was confused about how Sara and a few other friends had been avoiding her attempts to contact them. Jane seemed confused as she explained the situation to me.

As I sat there listening to the story, Jane made her case as to why she was in the right. She then asked me my view on the situation. I gave my view of what I heard, saying it was clear to me that she was wrong for the way she treated Sara. You may not agree with my initial assessment, but allow me to clarify my thought process. In my opinion, Jane wasn't wrong for her plans; she had made them months prior to her surgery. The surgery was an unplanned event that happened to fall around her training time. However, I felt that Jane was wrong for how she treated Sara, who came to help her during her surgery. As you can imagine, Jane didn't receive my view very well because she had an emotional attachment to her facts or what she perceived as fact.

Jane had no problem explaining the facts to me so I could agree with her, but when I gave an observation of how she possibly had done things wrong, or at least been a little insensitive to her friend, she was offended. Jane reiterated that she didn't ask Sara to come down. That was my issue with the situation; Jane didn't have to ask Sara for help. Sara, her friend, made an unselfish decision to come to her friend in a time of need and help any way she could.

Sometimes just saying that you are sorry can alleviate a lot of hurt that someone else is feeling over a situation. We have slowly become a society that thinks an apology shows weakness, but a healthy relationship can be destroyed because of pride. Acknowledging Sara for her generosity and informing her in advance of her plans would have probably been the best thing to do. When a person uses an excuse, it will come off the wrong way and seldom seem sincere. The excuse just makes it worse. Saying that she never asked her to come down just sounds mean, even though she may not have intended it to sound that way. Feeling unappreciated and used gave Sara a reason to disconnect communication from Jane, especially when she tried to help out of the kindness of her heart. When a person is hurt, some form of ex-communication or isolation will usually follow.

Common sense can be so clear when you apply it to someone else, but it can be evasive when you apply those same rules to your own situation. The discussion of lack of common sense is not to emphasize understanding men as much as it is for women to understand the bad decisions they may have made in their choices of men—what they have allowed men to do in their lives and why they have allowed it to continue.

Common sense is something that most people think they have, but they rarely use when it is required. I realize that the implementation of basic common sense can be based on your upbringing, past experiences, and current surroundings. Common sense can actually be relative in some cases because what one person thinks is common sense is not necessarily how someone else will see it.

I truly believe that there has to be some commonality with women as it pertains to a potential relationship with any man. To go into a relationship blindly is like walking into the street with a blindfold on. If you don't know what you want in a man, why pursue a man? Know what you want, be realistic, and work at the relationship together. Doing anything blindly can only be a testament of your overall expectation. Have you ever asked, "Why do I attract a certain type of guy in my life?" Better yet, "Why do I attract the wrong men in my life?" This is normally the type of man you are trying to avoid, right? Avoiding him may be more difficult than you think. Men can be like ticks; once they get their fangs into you, you need tweezers or fire to get rid of them.

You may not even be trying to attract the wrong man, but the wrong man seems to find his way to your door, quite similar to a stray hungry-looking dog that you see on the street. You will find that once you feed a hungry dog once, the dog will associate you with food and try to make you its supplier of food. The more you feed it, the more it comes back; the less you feed it, the less it's likely to keep returning. It could be as simple as your associations, neighborhood, or the selection of men you're exposed to on a daily basis. It could also be the very scent that you give off, which you may be unaware that you are excreting. The scent of your perfume could reek of desperation and your biological clock ticking. It could convey that you are tired of being alone. Whether or not you believe it, men oftentimes can smell that scent a mile away.

CHAPTER 4

A SIMPLE PHILOSOPHY

The original *Star Trek* show has seemed to endure the test of time, and it can still be seen in reruns on certain television stations today. It has also been made into several movies throughout the years. In the original *Star Trek*, there was a character named Mr. Spock. He was a Vulcan who displayed no emotions, and he was second in command behind Captain James T. Kirk. Captain Kirk was your typical emotional human who would jump into a situation headfirst, sometimes without thinking. The Vulcan society was known for their emotionless demeanor, and they displayed a very high level of intelligence through their "logical reasoning."

This level of reasoning seems to always be clouded by our emotional response to situations because we are creatures with emotions. Mr. Spock would oftentimes listen to Captain Kirk assessing a situation, and he was known for saying, "That is not logical" on many occasions while trying to understand the human thought process. Spock lacked emotions as a part of his decisions; his view was often a commonsense approach, which didn't factor his personal feelings into the equation.

He would compare the Vulcan way of thinking to the human way of understanding and responding to situations. By his mannerisms alone, he thought that his way of reasoning was much more superior to the human way of reasoning. Mr. Spock's reasoning was based on pure logic, without emotional interference. The problem with this way of thinking is that it can be seen as insensitive, but it was the core of what being a Vulcan is all about. Vulcans would make sound decisions that seemed logical and simple, without the emotional variance that humans used to come up with solutions. His judgment wasn't clouded by his emotions or feelings; it was simply guided by the pure facts of a situation.

You may be wondering why in the world I am talking about Captain Kirk and Mr. Spock, not to mention what a television show has to do with you. The main reason for this analogy is because as humans, our emotions drive the way we think, act, respond, and feel in situations. Sometimes our emotions drive us more than pure logic should. Our emotions sometimes cause us to make bad decisions that we would not normally make if our emotions were not a factor. But how do you separate emotions from a creature driven by emotions?

This is what made Mr. Spock's response to a situation so unique and easy for him; he had no emotional attachment to any situation brought before him. He based his decisions on the facts! Sure, he may have felt guilt, hurt, or pain in those decisions deep down inside when it came to his decision affecting his friends, but once he made the decision, he trusted in the logic. Now, by no means am I telling you to be like a Vulcan, without emotions, but I would suggest that you use your emotions when appropriate and use common sense when required. You have the ability to look at a situation and break it down to its lowest common denominator or basic common sense. We don't always do that, for there are so many factors that go along with our decisions. However, I am talking about protecting yourself from unnecessary pain. Again, I am not asking you to be emotionless but simply to recognize when emotions should be a factor and when they shouldn't. This will protect you from needless heartache.

I truly believe that Mr. Spock gauged himself more superior to his human colleagues because he felt that their emotions weakened their capacity to make sound decisions uncompromised by emotions when it counted. I know that using *Star Trek* as an example may seem silly, but it served a purpose, for Mr. Spock's emotionless Vulcan instincts were the best way to describe basic common sense and logical reasoning.

A decision made on the facts presented is something that takes time to effectively master without emotional influence, especially when it involves a relationship. The Vulcan analogy gave me a chance to expose what some women tend to do when a commonsense decision about a man needs to be made. Emotions get in the way even when your judgment and instincts are telling you otherwise. This is the time that a crucial mistake that can cost you dearly can be made concerning a man. Let me talk for a moment about common sense, for the use of those two words could offend some people because we all feel as if we have common sense. It is not my intent to offend but to make you truly think about decisions you have made that later made you wonder what in the world you were doing or thinking.

Common sense: *sound practical judgment*
Logical sense: *a system of reasoning*

Common sense can at times be in a constant battle with your emotions. It's not necessarily a bad thing; it's just reality, which can cause a lot of pain. You should never underestimate your emotions, for emotions will make you do something you know is wrong or foolish. This is why you may have often heard people say, "Never make a decision when you are emotional." This is when you are more vulnerable to making an error in judgment or an error in philosophy. This is when taking your time and allowing some time to pass before you make a decision is not a bad idea.

A philosophy error can be as simple as allowing the emotional pains of the past to make you think there is a shortage of quality men. Your philosophy is everything you know, and it affects how you think concerning a topic or situation, such as when you look at men and automatically think that men are intimidated by educated women and this is why you can't find the right one. You will say things like there are a shortage of good quality men or that all of the good men are taken. You may not even know it, but you may be justifying an ideal because you keep choosing the wrong man based on a bad philosophy.

The truth is that we are creatures who need answers to questions that seem to have no answer. When it becomes hard to explain something that is going wrong in your life, we can inadvertently create a reason even if the reason is not entirely accurate. A philosophy can turn into your attitude toward a topic or situation. So when you say that all men are dogs, what do you think your philosophy is toward all men?

Philosophy aside, I do not believe that a woman should lower her standards. If she has a vision of what she truly wants her man to be, there is nothing wrong with that concept. Remember also that standards are guides to help you when emotions can hinder your making a wise decision. In the standards that she uses, I believe that a woman should evaluate where her standards originated. Did those standards originate from a past hurtful relationship? Did those standards originate from what society says a man should be? Here is what I have noticed: in most cases, if you held yourself according to your own standards, you wouldn't be able to date yourself.

In my experience, some of the best husbands did not start out as husband material. They were not rich with the fancy car, the big home, or the large bank account; what they had was potential and a burning desire to be something more when no one else thought they could be. When you blame a man for the reason you are single, you give the man more power than he deserves. If you place the blame on the man, then you don't have to place the blame at your own feet. I have practiced that concept myself on many occasions, but I have learned that sometimes I may be the only reason for my unhappiness. Are you getting in the way of your own happiness? This all is a process that you must go through to allow you to weed out the wrong men without chasing away the right man.

The objective is to look for the man who has the will, desire, and ability to grow into a potential husband, if that is what you desire. If you have done your work, you have had to grow to be the woman that you are. A man who wants to become your soul mate and an equal partner with you will qualify himself if he is interested. He must earn the right to be the keeper of your heart.

You must understand that it is not the man's job to make you happy. This may not go over very well for some women, but this is an unrealistic expectation, and to keep it real, it is an unfair thing to place on a man. There should be a sense of excitement whenever you think about him or see him, but it is your responsibility to make sure that you are happy. I'm not speaking about the new excitement in the beginning of the relationship. After the initial infatuation stage has passed, does that excitement still exist? If not, you have the wrong view of what a relationship is all about, and maybe this is why you may be having difficulty finding the right man. You are so used to Buzz Lightyear that if his bells and whistles don't keep you excited, you lose interest and will focus on the negative.

You have to make yourself happy and understand that happiness has a short release cycle based on the current circumstances. Happiness is based on what is happening right now. If he isn't doing you right, then you are not very happy right now. If he loves you and can do no wrong, then you are very happy. Happiness can leave you up and down at any given moment, and you don't want to feel this most unpredictable emotion. What you want is joy, peace of mind, and contentment with the man you choose. Happiness is what causes women to gossip to their girlfriends and coworkers about what their man is not doing right rather than focus on what he does right. Happiness is temporary and based solely on circumstances. You need long-lasting joyful love, which will cause you to respect your relationship and keep your man's flaws between you and him, where they belong. I know that misery loves company, but never speak about your man in the company of another woman or especially another man. That is a recipe for disaster because a woman is most vulnerable when she is unhappy with her man.

The truth of the matter is that some of the best husbands are men you would not give a second look to because of their appearances, professions, or your perceptions. These are men who are hard workers, respect women, and people who would sacrifice anything for their families. They are the same guys you wouldn't give a second thought to if you saw them walking down the street. It begs this question: how do you know if he is not for you if you assume he is not for you?

Saying that takes me right into this: when someone, whether a man or a woman, is hurt emotionally, it's a paralyzing feeling. A woman can have new and improved standards that are developed as a safeguard from a past and hurtful relationship. When a woman puts her heart out there and it gets broken, she will tend to compensate by increasing her standards to avoid any chance of hurt in the future. She may start to feel an overwhelming sense of urgency for a meaningful relationship as each new relationship comes and goes with disappointment. The problem is that there will be more opportunities to be hurt with each passing relationship because she has to open up to that person. The more relationships that hurt your heart, the more you find yourself raising the bar on your standards as your heart starts closing. In the process, you are becoming hard and cold when it comes to relationships, and you have every right to feel that way, but the philosophy of how you view men that follows may do more damage than you realize.

This is the exact moment when it becomes difficult for any man to break down your defenses or penetrate your heart, especially if he happens to be the right man for you. The moment you start to protect yourself by closing your heart, you stop being who you really are and you become a harder version of the original you. Hurt knows no gender, age, or social class because hurt comes no matter how high you set your standards.

Whether it comes at you intentionally or accidentally, you can't avoid hurt. The concept is to learn and understand that hurt has to come in order for you to know what man is right for you. You should try to keep it to a minimum as much as possible without creating an impenetrable barrier in the process, but you will have to develop a touch skin when it comes to finding the right one. I understand protecting yourself from hurt, but you don't throw the baby out with the bathwater either. In other words, don't stop seeking the new man because of the last man. You have to learn from your hurt and not steal from the hurt. Do not steal your sensitivity, emotions, softness, and affection trying to compensate from being hurt the last time around. This will tend to destroy any relationships you will have with a new man, especially the right man. Make subtle changes and monitor your selection in a man the next time. That one man hurt you; not all men produced your hurt.

How do you minimize hurt from a bad relationship? Before you get into a relationship, know exactly what you are looking for and never rush into anything. The most important thing that seems to be missing from the list of things that a man should have is good character traits. Sure, I understand that women have wants and desires, and they range from emotional, physical, financial, and mental, but will the materialistic wants and desires really produce a fruitful and lasting relationship? Stop playing games with men who play games and get serious about what it is that you want in a man. Remember: you may not want it once you get it, so be very careful in what you ask for in a man.

I once knew a woman who said that when she was a little girl, she wanted a man who was a good provider. That concept came from what she saw as a little girl growing up and seeing how her own father was a great provider. The little girl grew up and married a man who was a good provider. You would think that she should be happy since she got exactly what she wanted since she was a little girl, right? The problem with that is that she stated that he was a lousy husband and his paternal skills could have used some fine-tuning. Unfortunately, there is more to being a good husband than just being a good provider. In the end, I got the feeling that she hated what she married because she realized that her wish as a little girl was the wish of a little girl and not the total package that a woman needs. Be careful what you ask for; you just might not want it when you get it.

If you ask a woman who doesn't really know what she wants in a man, you will often hear the cliché of a tall, dark, and handsome man. However, there is typically no mention of integrity, respect, protection, upbringing, and being a gentleman; moreover, his expression of love and basic communication usually isn't on that list. We all know that some men have trouble communicating in the most basic ways based on our upbringing, so that should be discussed.

You will want to set the tone for the type of man you want in your life. The tone has to be for the reasons that matter, not for the superficial reasons that never keep a couple together. The superficial reasons will tantalize the flesh in the beginning, but they will eventually damage your soul when they're over. For centuries, the chase after materialistic and vain things has been an aphrodisiac that has placed couples together for the wrong reasons. You should avoid falling into that trap because the end is still the same: divorce, heartbreak, and another failed relationship. You can't handle another bad relationship, broken heart, or risk building a relationship on a house of cards. If you are a woman reading this book, read with an understanding that every decision that you make does matter. If you are a man reading this book, read with the understanding of what you need to become to truly be a man she will be proud of.

CHAPTER 5

I WAS THE WRONG MAN

I titled the book *Your Choice in Men* because it is so important that women recognize when they are in the presence of one and for the men to recognize when they are one. In order to recognize when you have one requires taking responsibility for your decisions and knowing that you may have created your own misery. Sometimes fear is the culminating reason for allowing a guy into your life who shouldn't even be there. Simply put, it's not him; it just may be you. From a personal experience of mine, here is a good example of the wrong man and the fear of being alone.

In writing this book, I thought of a situation that I found myself in that I truly had to interpret as me being the wrong man. I quickly realized that there was more to me being the wrong man for this woman. She feared losing me and thought there wouldn't be anyone else after me. I enjoyed the attention, but I didn't consider her feelings and how my subtle rejection could be hurtful. You see, I was not really looking for someone to be in my life long term; I was still recovering from the emotional baggage that came from a recent divorce. I came home one day to find a note on my door saying that my neighbor wanted to get to know me better. I hesitated answering her because I knew that I wasn't ready for a relationship, but after listening to a female friend, I gave in and asked her out. The worst thing one can do is take advice from others and ignore your own voice, especially when you know that it can make things worse. As I said, although I wasn't looking for or was even ready for a relationship, I went against my instincts and responded to the note anyway, as my friend had suggested. I was curious, and a part of me just wanted to see what she looked like and why she was interested in me.

When I came to her door a few days later to meet her, I didn't know what to expect. When she opened the door, I noted that she was simply drop-dead gorgeous. She was nine years my senior, but you'd never know by looking at her. We got to know one another and had many conversations, but then as we shared more, I started to realize that she was looking for a significant other. I had no desire to be someone's significant other at that point in my life. I was always up front and honest with her and told her on several occasions that I wasn't ready for a relationship of that magnitude. The problem was that she didn't take no for an answer and

I wanted everything involved in a relationship without the actual relationship. This is how I knew that I was the wrong man for her; when a man thinks like this, he will hurt a woman emotionally. It doesn't matter that she suggested being friends with benefits; I knew that it was a bad idea, and I should have been more persistent with backing away in a way that would leave her with her emotional dignity. I just wanted to be friends, but it was difficult to be friends after the sexual tension hit its peak between us.

This woman did nice things for me to alleviate some of the stressors in my life. She tried to cook for me, she invited me out, and she gave me her spare key to her car so that if she lost her keys, at least she had a backup. These are things she definitely should have shared with the right man. I was benefiting from her generosity but taking advantage of it as well. I wasn't supposed to be receiving those types of pleasures, for I knew that I wasn't the right guy for her at that time. Once we entered into a sexual relationship, that's when everything changed.

We made an emotional connection sexually, and she even admitted she was using sex to change my mind about a relationship. I just wanted to be friends, but nothing she was doing would prevent me from thinking otherwise in spite of what I said. She went on a small quest to change my mind, which is a normal thing that some men and women do. The act of sex can create a hole that eventually will bring on hurt if you both aren't in it for the same reason. I started to actually change my mind about relationships, but that would have been the biggest mistake for me to do and for her to accept. I didn't want this relationship, and nothing I said could get me out of it because there was no easy way to tell her that I didn't want to be with her without hurting her feelings. Plus, if I didn't want to be with her, then why was I still in a sexual relationship with her? I asked myself that many times, and the only conclusion that I came up with was that she was fun, sexy, and attractive, whereas I was lonely and enjoying the attention by avoiding the commitment. Truth be told, I was wrong … and I was a man. I was the wrong man!

The truth can suck, but that was my truth at the time. I really didn't want to lead her on, and I was honest with her concerning not wanting a relationship, but my words were not matching my actions, so how did I expect her to interpret what I was doing? I accepted the food she cooked, and I came over and watched movies with her, only to be on the floor with her one-third of the way through the movie. I wasn't the typical jerk (wrong man) that women meet every day, because I actually cared about her feelings. It really didn't matter, because I was contradicting everything I said I didn't want.

I was trying to just be her friend, but we had moved past the friendship stage a long time ago. She was emotionally attached, and I was physically attracted, but that is not what a good relationship is all about. I tried to keep reminding her about the fact that I said from the beginning that I didn't want a relationship.

I then started to realize why she just couldn't let me go and why she was so emotionally attached to me. I had become the man that she had always wanted and I didn't even realize it at the time. It was about the non-committal companionship for me, but it was about the long-term relationship for her. I was selfish, and like so many men, I started to use the opportunities for selfish reasons. I had to come to the realization that while I was missing the companionship of a woman, I didn't want the relationship.

These dynamics that were happening were all wrong and caused so many problems that led to a terrible parting of the ways between the two of us. The point that I want to make here is that I had a conscience and was concerned about her feelings, but I was willing to engage in activities that would eventually lead to a scary situation for me in the end. I was actually involved with this woman while I was making final edits on this book. I was doing what I was actually writing about, and I was upset with my actions and myself.

I started to realize that the woman was actually scared. She was in her mid-fifties, and she thought that she would never find someone else if she allowed me to leave. I was doing everything she wanted a man to do in a relationship, and when you have that in your life, you will do and say anything to hold on to it. The concept was that if she allowed me to leave and I decide that I wanted to date again soon afterward, she would have missed her opportunity to be with me. The reality was that at this point in my life, I wasn't even close to what she wanted in a guy in areas that mattered. She wanted someone who was emotionally available to feel every essence of who she was as a woman, and I just wasn't there yet. I wasn't capable of doing that with her ... or any woman, for that matter. She started doing things that went against the things she wanted, like waiting for me, but waiting for me placed her in a miserable situation. Fear can be paralyzing, and in this instance, it paralyzed her more than she even knew or understood.

When I didn't do the things she thought I should do with her, like go out, stay up late, or stay overnight, she would often use words like that I was being mean, uncaring, and insensitive. I didn't understand it at the time, but I slowly started to realize that she was speaking from an emotional need that I was purposely withholding from her by only allowing the physical to manifest, without the emotional. I was doing what the wrong man does in so many instances, when he is only there for the physical pleasure and not there emotionally. Although I truly did not intend to hurt her, I was doing exactly that. The experience with me was creating the seed that would define how she viewed men after me.

When you are not in rhythm with people, you offend them mainly because you don't want the things that they want and you don't give them the things that they require.

That means the man will end up saying no to suggestions in many cases, which translates into negative feedback. Emotions are deep and tend to linger, so with someone who is emotional, any form of rejection can be extremely devastating.

Why did she accept the fact that my lack of emotional interest made her compromise what she really wanted in a man? She accepted what I wasn't giving her, because she thought I was everything she wanted in a man. She also accepted what I was giving her in the form of a penis because she thought I was everything she wanted in a man.

She stopped wanting a long-term relationship. She stopped wanting to spend quality time on weekends with the right man for her. She stopped wanting to travel on trips with the love of her life, just to spend time the way I was willing to give it to her at the time. I wasn't able to be a part of those things she wanted, for I was emotionally unavailable and had other wants during that time in my life. She did what so many women do: she put what she wanted on hold just to be in the presence of a man who didn't want the same things she wanted.

It's wasn't that I didn't necessarily want the same things she wanted. I just wasn't able to appreciate those things at that moment because, if you remember, I was recently divorced at the time and needed to deal with the aftermath of a failed relationship. The reality for me was that I was more interested in making my ex-wife see that I had moved on than I was interested in becoming a man this woman could fall in love with at the time. She stated at the beginning that she wanted a long-term relationship, and I was looking to show my ex-wife that I wasn't broken. I know that sounds selfish and cruel, but it is rather common for someone to do when dealing with the emotions of a failed marriage or lost love.

After the healing process starts to take hold, you tend to do things that you would regret under a sound mind. The problem is that hurt people tend to hurt other people, and that is exactly what I was doing. What was really happening in this situation was that she knew what she wanted in a man; the problem was that I wasn't ready to be that man because I was emotionally unavailable and still in love with my ex-wife. She started to compromise everything she told me that she wanted by doing what she really didn't want to do. When I looked up, I realized that I was the wrong man for her, even if it was hard for me to admit it. When you are the wrong man for a woman, you have the ability to destroy the very fiber of what makes that woman strong and confident.

Chapter 6

HIS NATURE

If you want a relationship with a man, you will need to deal with the nature of that man. A relationship with any man goes well beyond the fakeness of the dating process. I think this is where mistakes are made in most situations. When you date a guy, he will usually be on his best behavior, so you are not actually meeting the man but rather his representative. You will receive flowers, candy, and dinners at nice restaurants. He will open the car door for you, and you will receive compliments as you two get to know each other. The problem is that with all this nice treatment, none of it is real in the sense that this is what he does every day.

You don't know how this man treats a woman after a few years of familiarity with that woman. Do you know how this man responds to pressure? A pressure situation will expose an anger problem or a hitting problem. You need to study a man under pressure so you know how he will react in certain situations. When under extreme pressure, will he curse you or resort to abusive behavior? You will need to look deeper at the total man and not the representative that is sitting across from you at the dinner table.

Simply put, the nature of a man is the language of a man. We know that men and women talk differently, but we have yet to understand why that is. Boys and girls grow up differently in how they interact, communicate, and play with others. Girls will normally be able to speak full sentences before a boy can even muster up the word daddy. Girls are taught that it's all right to show their emotions, while boys are told to hide their emotions and be like a man. Boys will typically play in the dirt, play rough with other boys, and play with toy trucks and cars. Girls, on the other hand, will often play with baby dolls and Easy Bake Ovens. Boys will fall down and skin their knee, while girls will try to play in dresses, all the while being told periodically to be careful not to fall down because they may get their clothes dirty.

This is where it all starts, where the gap widens between girls and boys, communication and no communication. That may be why the men in your life have not been able to express themselves; they possibly grew up hearing and understanding that it's not manly to express their emotions freely without ridicule. This also may be why the men in your life have not been helpers around the house, for while you were learning to take care of your baby doll and cooking in your Easy-Bake Oven, the boys were playing outside with their friends. There is not much of a sense of responsibility in that when you look at it from how boys are sometimes raised. Then as boys grow up to be men, we expect them to be responsible and express their emotions, but they often don't have the skills to comprehend what that means.

Is it really that important to know how a man thinks in order for you to be happy or find true love? I truly believe that you can only be responsible for your own life and how you think, respond, and react in situations. If you have a set of standards that are nonnegotiable, things you will and will not accept in a relationship, then I truly believe that you are creating an environment for a true man to manifest himself in your life.

It makes no sense to waste your time trying to think like a man when you have never been one. Just stick to thinking like the smart and intelligent woman that you are and make better and wiser decisions when it comes to men. You can't control a man—so stop reading books that make you think you can. You can read all the books in the world and you will still go to your grave trying to answer the question of how men think about relationships, women, money, dating, sex, and cheating.

Truth be told, although I'm a man, I sometimes don't know how I feel about these same topics on any given Sunday. There are several people who may disagree with me, but I will say that the only time you need to know how a man thinks is if you are a man. The problem with trying to understand men is that you will typically have to place all men in the same category. That is great if all men were the same in all areas, but realistically you and I both know that that is just not the case.

I would recommend that you resist the temptation to fall for the garbage that all men are the same. It sells books, but common sense should tell you that it isn't true. I believe that trying to understand how men think was not meant for you as a woman to figure out. If you think a woman is complicated, you can't even imagine how complicated a man can be within his own head at times. The misconception that men are simplistic creatures is something that will cause you to misjudge your own man; he has many layers that you have yet to see.

The only thing that you as a woman need to remember is that you can only control what you do and what you think. I have heard countless hours of women trying to understand why men do what they do. You would think that through all the conversations around the world and all the technology to unravel information that surely we would have an answer to this timeless question concerning what men are thinking and why they do what they do.

Common sense will tell you that men think differently about different things depending on each man's past, present, and future experiences, as is the case with you. You will be wrong in most cases if you think you know what a man is thinking or even if you try to guess. Again, certain books can plant the misconception that all men are the same. But consider the following. If all men are the same, then would it be fair to say that all women are the same too? If all men are the same, then what difference does it make concerning which man you choose? If all men cheat, then you'd be better off picking the cutest cheater and have a great life with this guy. All men are not the same, nor do they think the same, but you may be in the same dysfunctional cycle when it comes to every man in your dating circle.

It is very important that you do not blame all men because of your bad decisions in choosing a man. I know that there are some bad men out there, and you will have one run up on you eventually, but it is more important that you know what you will allow in your life short term before you think about a long-term relationship. Is your dating circle dysfunctional? Are you dysfunctional in your choices of men?

Understand that the average man is meant to be in your life for a very short period of time in order for you to practice your standards. There are a very small percentage of men that are actually meant to be in your life for longer than six months. If you have no concrete standards in place that you follow, then those men who are meant for a short period will linger for long periods and ruin your perception of what men are. That slight error in judgment will cause you to speak badly about men in general, just as your girlfriend's likely do at work about their men or husbands. It is not the man's fault. It is your fault for not being resolute in what you will and will not accept from men. If you accept trash, you get a trashy man who will be the architect of your trashy relationship.

If a man calls you the B-word, you immediately know that he is not the one for you. That is overtly understandable, but it is the subtle things that you may have trouble seeing and withdrawing from. It is the subtle things that slowly chip away at your emotions, which will make it harder each time to kick this guy to the curb. You do not need to know what men think; it has everything to do with what you will allow a man to do to your body, emotions, and your will.

When people say that all men are the same, I often wonder exactly what they are referring to. Could it be that when a woman says that all men are the same, she is speaking from a personal place of hurt that she has now transferred over to all men based on the one man who hurt her, especially if she had more than one man hurt her in a particular way that is familiar to her? When you have a man come in and literally swoop you off of your feet and treat you like someone special, it makes you feel unbelievable. When this same man disappoints you by cheating, abusing, or hurting your heart, it affects how you feel and view every man that comes after him.

Can you predict or control what your man will do at any given moment? Probably not! Whether you believe it or not, men need to feel that you respect them. I will always suggest that the only thing that matters is that you show him that you love him and respect him. You may not always get back the level of love you give, but you can only control what you can control. You always have the option of not accepting a relationship that lacks the reciprocation of emotion, respect, and love. You can always choose to leave, but the point is that you need to figure out what it is that you want and need from a man. You will also need to decide what you want and need from a relationship and what you can contribute to the relationship to sustain those expectations.

Let's use an example to make another point. I was watching a court show on TV the other day. On the show, the plaintiff was a white female and the defendant was a white male. The race of the people is not important, but I want to paint a clear picture for you. The woman started off by saying that she and the gentleman got an apartment together. The apartment was in her name because he had bad credit (red flag number one). He wasn't able to get them an apartment as her boyfriend and couldn't even have his name on the lease (red flag number two). She also went on to say that he was unemployed at the time and owed back child support (red flag number three). Do you see a pattern here?

The judge looked at her and said, "So you knew going in that he was a financial risk and you got an apartment with him anyway?" The woman responded, "Yes ma'am!" The look on the judge's face said that she couldn't believe what she was hearing. I actually mumbled under my breath the word "stupid"! The judge told her to continue with her reasons for being in court. You can probably tell that it had to do with money and the apartment. Needless to say, the woman finally saw the light after the damage had been done. The judge eventually threw the case out and told her to consider it a lesson learned.

When you read this short reenactment, it may be clear to you that the woman made a bad decision concerning this guy. Most people can see that right off the bat without hesitation because they are viewing this without any emotional attachment to it. This was a decision that someone with your intelligence level would never make under any circumstances … right? But wait a minute—it was clearly apparent to me that this woman thought and said the same thing about herself that you are likely saying about yourself. I wondered to myself what made her common sense thinking malfunction in this particular case.

I want to submit to you that she was not thinking clearly, because she was trying to fulfill a need for love, sex, companionship, or something deeper, without looking at this from a common sense approach. Let's evaluate her scenario and weigh her options for a moment. The man that she was dating was unemployed and gave no real reason to the judge as to why he wasn't working. He owed back child support to a woman who had a child by him. His credit was so bad that he could not even put his name on a lease for an apartment; his girlfriend had to do it for him. The first thing that comes to mind is, *What was she thinking?* Right? This goes back to my initial statement of your not needing to know what a man is thinking; you only need to know what you are thinking.

So let's break this one down systematically. One theory is that he was probably unemployed because he didn't want to pay child support. This is a tactic that is commonly used by guys, and I was only aware of it because a childhood friend was doing the same thing at one time. It seems a bit extreme just to avoid child support, but a man will go to extreme lengths to avoid doing something he doesn't want to do. I believe that this guy had no intentions of supporting his child, which should have been an obvious sign about his character. I figured that he either had questions about the child's paternity or he and the mother didn't get along and this was a form of payback. The reality is that this man had no desire to take care of his child, which lets me know that he was absolutely the wrong man for this woman. There is no reason that a woman would risk everything to be with a man with a character that is the opposite of what she needs.

She was not using her common sense, but as I have stated, "common sense is not that common." He had bad credit, which kept him from even renting an apartment of his own. He didn't have a job to help pay for the apartment, but on top of all of that, his credit was just like him … no good! Is this the man she was looking to make her dreams come true? He will certainly be in her dreams, but it will be a nightmare.

The common sense approach would be to truly look at what you want from a man and stop compromising your standards. He is not the only man in the world, so there is no reason to think that there is no one else out there for you. Patience is not a sin when it comes to finding the right man; it's the key to common sense.

CHAPTER 7

A WOMAN IN CONTROL

A woman has total control over what man she wants in her life. The old adage comes into play that with control comes responsibility, and making good quality decisions is a by-product of control. The way in which you choose a man will inherently separate you from the women who have chosen wrong or too quickly and then spent years recovering from lost time, broken hearts, and emotional baggage.

For the most part, I believe that men spend the majority of their adult lives making up for lost time. The average woman has spent her years growing up warding off the unwanted advances of young boys from the time of grade school to college. By the time she has become an adult, she is so tired of the same old advances from boys who are now men that she is hardened by the thought of it. The average boy doesn't receive that type of attention as a youth and then grows up to be a handsome young man and then experiences attention from girls and women on a level he is not necessarily used to receiving.

When you think about it from a man's perspective, from how we view the dating arena, a man will spend the majority of his dating life asking to be a part of the life of a woman that he happens to be interested in. As a woman, you get the unique opportunity to choose whom you desire to spend your time with and get to know. If you don't believe me, go to any club or social event that has men and women. You will see the guys trying to spark conversations, asking for telephone numbers, attempting to purchase drinks, and trying to impress young women. The choice is yours, ladies, but have you misunderstood the ability to choose?

This is a decision that can at times be taken for granted, but if your decision of a man is wrong, you could essentially go through the worst relationship and experience of your life. If the decision and choice is right, then you will have the opportunity to live a life that is as close to "happily ever after" as we can have on this earth.

So why does the decision to choose the right man for you seem to be such a difficult thing to do? There can be several reasons, but one of those could be that you already know that your decision in that man is wrong in the first place; however, you may feel that you are making this decision for the right reasons. It is so easy to get caught up in what I call the "STOPP" of most men. This is an acronym for the sex, (*s*), the tangibles (*t*), and the over exaggerated promise of potential (*opp*).

The Sex

Men have a lot of things to offer women, but the problem can often be that what a particular man is offering is something you just don't need right now in your life, no matter how good it feels. Men can certainly offer you sex, but so can a dog when he humps your leg at the dinner table. The thought of your getting with a man just for sex sounds unreasonable on the surface, but sexual desire is a very strong emotion, and it's not uncommon for that to be the driving force in wanting a relationship. We are all human, and the majority of people, including myself, have probably done this at least once in their lifetimes. The feeling that you get from sex is probably the best feeling you will ever experience when it comes to body stimulation. Sex brings two people closer, relieves stress, and is a way of bonding two lovers in a way that nothing else can do. However, when you have sex with someone you are not supposed to be with, you create a world that is not the true reality of the world you were designed to operate within.

The need for sex can be very strong for you, especially when you haven't had it in a while and you are feeling weak. This is when you may do things you wouldn't do if you were in your right mind, such as sleep with people you normally wouldn't. In other words, I believe that sexual frustration can make you literally lose your mind and forget that you have standards. I suggest that you never underestimate the pull that sex can have on you, because this is the hardest area to resist. You should know that if you compromise in this area, you will not be happy in the long run and it will lead to a lot of unfulfilled experiences. Notice that I didn't say relationship.

The Tangibles

What a man has when it comes to material belongings can attract a woman and give her the appearance that there is substance. Men will often acquire those tangible materialistic things in order to get the woman. It's kind of like the guy who buys the nice car to attract women, but little do you know that he may be sleeping in his car. Most guys believe that the car, house, clothes, and jewelry that he acquires will to some degree attract a woman. For the most part, some of those men may be correct. The question remains: what type of woman will they attract? You can never be that woman who is drawn in by the hollow trappings of success. If you are looking for true happiness, it will not come wrapped in a car or house but in a long-standing relationship with someone who loves you more than he loves himself.

Over exaggerated Promise of Potential

A promise is only valid when you have corresponding actions to go with it. A promise is your word, and your word should produce fruit. Potential is something that a person can foresee happening in the future based on constant and consistent preparation. Ladies, if you don't see him preparing consistently based on his promise, then don't expect the potential to manifest anytime soon. I'm not saying that he doesn't have potential, but his potential will always be based on what he is doing rather than what he is saying.

When a man tends to over-exaggerate a promise of potential, it's probably because you have placed a demand on him that he knows he is unable to produce right now. A man will typically do this as a form of stalling until he figures out another way to keep you around and deflect your attention from what you are asking from him. When a woman is in an abusive relationship and she threatens to leave her man, he will often present her with an over exaggerated promise of potential. He will tell her, "I promise to never put my hands on you again." There is no reason for you to believe that statement, because you haven't seen any corresponding actions to go with that promise of potential. If he hasn't sought any form of help from a counselor, pastor, or a program that specializes in this area, then why would you believe his promise? If he hasn't admitted to you that he has a problem, then there should be no reason to believe anything that is said. He will then do something nice for you or buy you something as a peace offering in an attempt to make the situation go away. This will normally work, and you will assume that he has finally changed, until the next argument.

A woman can give a person like this the benefit of the doubt because she is hoping that for her benefit, there is a true change in his behavior. I have seen this with my own eyes, especially when she truly loves him. Women are nurturers, lovers, and typically more trusting, so it's not a surprise when a woman gives a guy a fifth and sixth chance. I will end this segment with this: you can't afford the luxury of blindly trusting a promise of potential if you do not see the corresponding preparatory actions. You have to trust what your eyes are telling you, so if you don't see him doing anything to change, then he probably isn't changing. In some cases, how much you trust could mean your life, and in most cases, you can waste valuable time on a guy who is not ready to change and definitely is not interested in changing for you.

Chapter 8

BLAMING YOURSELF WON'T BE EASY

Who's to Blame?

When you make the wrong decision when it comes to choosing a man, the implications can be devastating. What I am about to say next may not go over so well, but I honestly believe it will give insight. When this type of devastation occurs in your life, I find it hard to always blame the man when he wasn't meant for you in the first place. If you are not careful, you will blame the man for a bad decision that you made when you chose someone you thought was the right one based on superficial reasons. You will soon find that he was not worthy to be the keeper of your heart, but it will take a broken heart for you to realize it. The fact of the matter is that most men are not qualified to be the keeper of your heart, so it may not always totally be his fault when it doesn't work out. It is actually your fault. The keeper of your heart is not something that you hand over to a man without forethought, because a lot of responsibility comes with that position.

When you make a decision about a man, you are inviting into your life whatever is good and whatever is bad that he is bringing to the table. When you choose someone for the wrong reasons, you have to accept responsibility for that bad choice. The wrong man will always bring everything that is wrong because you were not supposed to be with him in the first place. The responsibility has to fall at your feet and no one else's, for the wrong man will do what he is designed to do—bring you everything wrong. Do not ignore the part that you played in inviting that type of guy into your life.

When you find the right man, it takes a lot of work to stay together even under the best conditions, for life is challenging and people change. I would advise that if you are going to go through challenging times, do it with the right man, the one who is the keeper of your heart, not the wrong guy, who doesn't care about your heart.

The Basics

Whatever happened to common sense? Don't cross the street before looking both ways—common sense. Don't accept a ride from a stranger—common sense. Don't leave a club by yourself with a man you just met—common sense.

Don't have unprotected sex with a man you barely know— common sense. This last one is performed more than you may realize. You should not be so quick to give your heart to every man you meet just because he tells you that he loves you.

Protecting your heart requires sound judgment, diligence, and mother-hen protecting instincts. You want to make sure that you do not punish a good man for the mistakes of the wrong man. You will have to learn to leave your past in the past and move forward toward your future. You don't want to get into the habit of exposing your heart to a man who is not deserving of that exposure.

How do you protect your heart? You must protect your heart by making emotionless decisions when it comes to love and relationships in the beginning. How do you make emotionless decisions? You don't fall in love at first sight! You don't say that you love a man until you are sure why you love him! You ask all the questions and get all the answers. You will also need to meet his family and ask all the questions and get all the answers that will be necessary to understand where this man originated. You will need to visit his apartment or place of residence to get a sense of who this man is when he relaxes. You must be clear as to what you want in a man, those things that have nothing to do with his money, status, or sexuality. You must also be clear as to who this man is before you become all caught up in the aura of his presence. A man with a good character, morals, and values is far more valuable than any amount of money a man can offer you as a part of a relationship.

Rich people get divorced all the time, which proves that money will not keep a couple together. It all goes back to marrying for the wrong reasons, and the consequences of doing so will always show themselves in the end. A relationship that is built on a lie will not always fall apart because of the particular lie that was told but because it creates mistrust within the relationship. When trust is lost, the relationship is lost. The longevity of a relationship only exists at a level of compatibility that is deeper than monetary or vain reasons.

If you don't correct your flaws now, you will find yourself repeating the same relationship cycle and making excuses for why it didn't last. Common sense will minimize silly mistakes, but it won't eliminate those silly mistakes that hinder a relationship. I ask that you allow me to show you how common sense can help you stop trying to understand men but rather start understanding when to use your emotional response when it is appropriate and when to use your common sense when it is required.

Emotional Control

If you find yourself in a situation where a man with whom you are deeply in love with did you wrong, whether it was by cheating on you or whatever the situation, the first thing you need to do is be emotional. I know that may contradict the heading "Emotional Control," but we are emotional creatures and an element of emotions are uncontrollable. When it comes to a relationship, hurt, pain, and insensitive actions will come in different forms. You can find yourself hurt by actions that are intentional and unintentional, but you will need to express the hurt that you feel in a constructive way. Crying is an obvious way to express your emotions, while anger is a close second and can even come in first most of the time. You should always give yourself permission to be angry, cry, scream, yell, and pray, but make sure that you do this in private. There are moments during times of weakness that privacy is your friend and your strength at the same time, and these are the moments that you will experience it.

This is an interesting generation that we live in because men will mirror violence more than ever, especially with women. I suggest that you never allow your temper to get the best of you and act out in violence toward a man. The best way to handle a situation that involves massive and emotional pain is to understand that a man responds to strength and reacts to weakness. I am not saying that this transition of emotion will be easy, but it will be of benefit to you in the end.

A reaction is typically an expressive impulse that can be very unpredictable. The problems around having an unpredictable reaction are just that—your actions are unpredictable. This is why I suggest that you handle your moments of weakness in private, for you will be in an unpredictable state. If you approach your man in an unpredictable state of mind, you will place him in an unpredictable state as well. Once you gather your thoughts and get yourself together, then you will be able to approach the situation from a state of strength. When people respond to something, they have some forethought and their expressions will be calculated and precise. You will always want to maneuver from a position of strength because this will allow your man to maneuver from the same state of mind. A man will respond to strength, and his response will be calculated and coordinated.

There are many variables concerning information that has to be taken into account. Not all information is true so consider the source of any information when it comes to your man. You must also make sure that you eliminate hearsay and stick to the facts concerning what you know. You will find that you will have better control and will be fully capable of handling any situation. If you come to a person in a state of anger, then you will find that you are capable of doing anything when you are emotionally charged and out of control. You can be emotionally out of control in private, but you can't afford to do that with your man. You already know that you will have a strong urge to rush in and confront him about the situation, but it's best to resist this feeling as often as possible. No matter how much you tell yourself that you've got this, you *will* be out of control at some point during the confrontation … Trust me on this one. There is nothing viler than for a woman to be out of control when she is trying to get answers. At the end of the day, you will not get the answers you seek; you will simply leave the situation with more questions.

When you are out of control, you do not think straight and you are prone to make the wrong decisions initially that you will regret in the end. You are a lady! You are a queen! You must be a *controlled* emotional wreck. You will have to redefine yourself emotionally in order to get to this level of interaction. You will have to work on self-development in order to be able to conquer the urge to go off.

A woman, by nature, will be more emotional than most men are. In the area of infidelity, women often cry, shout, and seek the comfort of other women who can empathize and sympathize with her. There are times when you may withdraw yourself from your friends and family for a reasonable period of time because of the embarrassment and hurt.

Once you have gone through all of your emotions, you must now use common sense and retain control of your emotions. Alternatively, there are women who find out that their men are cheating and they want to fight the other women or attack their men. That is an example of being an out-of-control emotional wreck. I am sure you will be the first to admit that there are women who are very emotional anyway, so to express your displeasure through that avenue is a recipe for disaster and a grave mistake. When emotional expression turns violent or excessive, it becomes counterproductive, annoying, and creates an environment for retaliation.

Love Is a Gamble

Love is a gamble, and you will lose more than you win, but just because the odds are not in your favor, it doesn't mean you lose your mind and give up. The odds are supposed to be against you. It is hard work finding someone who will love you until death do you part. When you think of loving someone until death, what you are saying is that you are going to love someone no matter what happens, which includes the ultimate highs and the lowest of lows. It is hard work finding someone who will love you in spite of your faults, flaws, and quirky hang-ups.

It is never easy finding someone who will love you no matter what happens, because we can be selfish creatures at times, only thinking about how our mates' health will affect us. This is not a movie where you live happily ever after. This three-dimensional life will knock you down, kill your dreams, and make you barricade your heart because someone hurt you in the past. Just because you got hurt once, twice, or six times doesn't mean you quit seeking and searching. You just seek and search smarter each time.

You just have to learn from your mistakes by reviewing your past actions and using better common sense. What sense does it make to quit on love? In my book, it makes no sense in the world! One thing is for sure: if you stop looking for love, you will never find it. Short-term pain for long-term gain takes strength and common sense.

When angry, it makes no sense trying to slash his tires, attempting to stab him, or kicking his family tree in the ass for creating him. I understand the concept, but what would it accomplish? You would be in jail and passed around the cell like a cheap cigar while he is still sleeping around with other women. You must mark it down as a bad decision on your part for choosing that man—and choose better the next time.

You have to learn emotional control through emotional practice. You learn control through self-development. You have to learn control by being in situations that should cause you to be out of control. You must be provoked in most cases in order to know that you are able to stay in control. If you really want to know how to be in control, you must seek the tools in order to do what you seek. Everyone has a breaking point, but you can choose to react differently once you have matured in this particular area.

CHAPTER 9

CHANGE YOURSELF, NOT HIM

If your mother never told you this when you were a little girl, then you need to call her up and ask her why she didn't. The biggest mistake a woman can make is thinking that she can change her man. A man will change only when he is consciously aware that there is a need for him to be better. Until a man is consciously aware that he needs to make a change, he will not change just because you think you can make him change. I repeat: he *will not* change just because you think you can make him change. This has been hard for women I've known to understand, so I had to say this twice.

The second mistake is made when some women go into relationships with their eyes shut and their hearts wide open. Consider the saying "Follow your heart." You can use that mantra if you want, but you will find yourself all over the place. You need to lead your heart and stop following your heart, because your heart may be subject to following some weird, rough, and stupid men. Lead your heart, and tell your heart which way to go and whom to love.

In the old-school days, going into a relationship by following your heart may have been the way to go because a man's word was his bond back in the day. A man typically would not leave his family under any circumstances, because in most cases, he was the sole breadwinner. Being a man was honorable, and being a father came with a sense of responsibility and commitment. Some people may be too young to remember this, but men made business deals with a handshake, and their honor was judged by what they said during the handshake. The handshake and their word was the binding contract that sealed many business and personal deals. In most cases, your word was all you had. I find that as I get older, I've noticed a different generational mind-set toward the role that a man plays within the family. There are men out there whose word is not as binding as it once was so many years ago, nor is the commitment to his family.

With all of that being said, the protection of your heart in the beginning of a relationship is very much on you. Even under ideal and perfect situations, you are subject to getting your heart broken, but the key is to minimize unnecessary heartbreak over guys who should not be in your life in the first place. You must consciously protect your heart and emotions until you decide that the man you are dealing with is worth the effort of opening up. When you open up your heart, remember to do it slowly, not like the legs of a two-dollar hooker. When the man proves that he is worthy of your love, then the protection of your heart falls on him. Nevertheless, you must understand that he may still hurt you unintentionally, but knowing that if his heart is in the right place, he will learn from his mistake and not do further damage can be reassuring.

When a woman enters a relationship, everything is fresh and new. The sun shines brighter, the birds sing at her window, and he looks like a knight in shining armor. The problem is that when you are in the entry stages of love, you are at the purest and most emotionally honest that your heart will ever be in during the relationship. If he is not the guy for you, all the signs to drop him like a hot potato are there, but you may find that you ignore them for the need of what I call "romanticism of love."

I will explain the term with a simple example. The man you are dating may have a child for whom he owes back child support. You notice that he has no real intentions to pay and he blames the mother for his reasons for not paying. I understand that some women do use child support for personal and selfish reasons that have nothing to do with the child, but I am talking about the mind-set of fatherly responsibility of your man. Let's continue …

He has horrible credit because of his inability to manage his finances. He doesn't have a job but talks about getting one, with no real action behind his words. This example is extreme but not that far off from the men that you will meet out there.

Now, my question to you would be this: what makes you think a man like this would be responsible enough to be the keeper of your heart? You're probably in love with a man like this because he is cute, fine, gorgeous, or whatever adjective you use to describe his features. You may be in love because it's been a long time since you felt this way about someone and you are a woman with needs—right?

You may be in love with him because you hear your biological clock ticking and you want a man to help you have a baby. (On a side note, your biological clock is not a logical reason to step out blindly and commit emotional suicide with someone who only wants you for short-term reasons.)

You may be in love with him because you love the feeling of being in love, no matter whom you love. You may be in love with him because he is all you know or have ever known. Finally, you may be in love with him because you are ready to get married. None of these excuses are valid, but they all are used to justify your love for the skanky man you are choosing to be the keeper of your heart.

He was a player when you met him, so now you want to marry the player and then you have the audacity to be surprised when he plays around on you with other women. This is not an example of good common sense, but this is an everyday occurrence that we make as people. Change

your approach to men and stop trying to change the man …
Change yourself.

To think that you can change a man who doesn't even
attempt to change himself is a recipe for emotional and
relationship disaster. I do believe that this saying is nothing
new, but it seems as though there is a process that has to
be taken until this sticks as reality. A man will not change
until he sees an absolute reason for the need to change and
become a better person. This can be sparked by tragedy,
enlightenment, conversion, or his just plain being tired of
himself and his ways. If you do not come to understand that
you can't change a man in and of yourself, this will be the
start of a never-ending cycle with you getting emotionally
involved with the wrong men. You will eventually ask
yourself at some point when the relationship ends, "Why
do I always attract the wrong men?" Better yet, the question
you should be asking yourself is, "Why did I make a bad
decision to be with a man I knew was wrong for me?"

I am an animal lover, and I have traditionally favored
cats as pets over the years, even though I love dogs too.
I have had only female cats as pets because they seem to
be softer in demeanor and countenance than their male
counterparts. The one thing I have noticed about cats is that
they make you work for their affection on a daily basis; dogs
just want to please their owners. There is nothing wrong
with a dog wanting to please its owner, but that's not the
point I want to make here. To the naked human ear, a cat's

meow sounds the same from cat to cat. But to the owners, their cats' meows can be clearly differentiated from other cats. It is a distinct sound to them, even when the cats look alike. One main reason is because even though all cats may have the same mannerisms, each cat responds and speaks to its owner differently. My point is that men may look alike, sound alike, and act alike on the surface, but every man is distinct and different in his own unique way … if you are willing to watch and listen.

Ask yourself these three simple questions to see if you have a starting point as it relates to men:

1. What standards do you have for yourself?
2. What will you allow a man to bring into your life?
3. Will you be willing to walk away from a man if he compromises your core values?

These are all valid questions that need real answers from you. You are the only one who can answer, enforce, or violate the answers to these questions. If you want someone to love you unconditionally, it would probably be best if you invested your money in buying a dog. Dogs are known as man's best friend because they will love you no matter what you do, with no conditions attached. If you want a life partner, you must practice your standards because men only respond to the level of respect you show toward yourself. A man will spend money for a freak in the night of darkness, but only a respectable woman will meet his mother.

Why do you think a man loves his mother so much? Is it because she demands to be loved in a certain way by her son and over the course of time, he is conditioned to love? She probably gave him guidelines and standards that she was not going to be disrespected by him at any time in his life. She likely enforced that he would love her and she would love him no matter what he did. He was told that you only get one mother so you'd better treat her right. He was conditioned to treat his mother in a certain way. If you do not condition your man to love you a certain way, then that man will condition you to accept anything in the name of apathy. What have you required from your man lately?

A mother's love will make a son do anything to defend her honor. As a boy growing up in a small country town in Virginia, we would joke with each other, or "play the dozens," as it is sometimes called. The unwritten rule was that you *could not* talk about anyone's mother. You could talk about daddies, but mom was off limits. If someone joked about your mother, you were ready to fight over it even if it meant getting beat up. You must learn to demand that same type of respect from men, but you can't do that when men think you're an easy booty call with little persuasion. Truth be told, the average man will accept a late night booty call from you, but that same man will probably not consider you wife material because of that same reason.

Your House Shouldn't Be Every Man's Home

The one word that you should take from this section is "categorize." Whether you believe it or not, men place women in all kinds of categories all the time. You may be the booty call. You may be the freak. You may be the she-crazy-as-hell woman. You may be the gold digger. You may be the Monday through Friday, just not the weekend girl. You may be the weekend girl, but not Monday through Friday. You may even be the church girl that will fornicate on the side. Trust me when I say that you are in some man's category somewhere, whether you know it or not.

The only question that remains is this: if you had to categorize yourself, which woman are you? If you are true to yourself with your answer, you might be unhappy with your answer right about now. The good thing is that this is the time to make a change within yourself. Categorizing is what men do, and they work you based on how they see you. And yes, I said that men work you based on how they see you, not by how you see yourself.

Have you ever wondered why men are good at games like football and basketball? The goal is to win no matter what it takes, to come in first and to beat any opponent who is after the prize. It is the competition of man against man, and the objective is to win. A relationship can imitate a game at times if you look at it in a unique way. When a man tries to win your love from another or just for him, it is a part of a romantic game between two people. As a woman, you play hard to get, even when you like him, because you don't want to seem too easy. He acts as if he has it all together when he probably lives with his mother, is lying about his age, and is trying to impress you with flowers and his car that he can't afford. It's all a game—a cute love game, but still a game.

The hardest thing will be for me to get you to admit that you categorize people all the time. The second hardest thing will be to get you to be open to admit to yourself that there could possibly be some truth in what I am saying.

This is what I want to bring to the table. Categorize the men in your life outside of your immediate family and generate or revive a set of hard-core values and standards that you will and will not accept under any circumstances. If you want to play Russian roulette with relationships, then do not let me stop you. This book may not be for you. But if you are looking for a true relationship and you truly believe that you attract the wrong men in your life, then keep reading.

You must always remember that not every man is meant for you! It's a numbers game. Numerically, you will meet more wrong men than you will meet right men, and that is the way it was designed. So understand that by nature, the wrong man is supposed to do what wrong men do—turn you off. That is why we call them the wrong men in your life. What you have possibly done is try to turn the wrong man into the right man against his will.

There is no special cave or laboratory chamber that holds the belongings to your right man. Good men are not like roaches, hiding in a crack and waiting for the lights to go out before they appear. If you have not met every man in the world regardless of his skin color, you haven't gone through them all. What is funny is that you have probably met a good man before but you didn't even recognize him.

Chapter 10

THE RACE CARD

I have noticed that there are a few women out there who have been hurt by men of a certain ethnicity group. I say ethnicity group because that hurt has caused them to consider eliminating that group and exclusively sticking with another group as potential men that they would be willing to date. I do agree with the notion that the man who makes you happy should not be predicated on what color he is but how he makes you feel about yourself when you are with him. The problem that I have is the notion that assuming that a certain ethnic group of men is better than others is a flawed concept. The thought is that a certain ethnicity of men will treat you better in a relationship compared to the current ethnicity that hurt you is not a proven concept. The essence of a man is decided within; it is not decided by the color on the outside. How a man treats you is totally based on what you don't see that has been groomed inside of his spirit, but remember that it will never be seen within the pigmentation of his complexion.

I am closely familiar with certain ethnicities that say they are dating white men exclusively because of the hurts rendered by their previous ethnic relationships. I certainly understand the point and feelings behind why someone would make this statement, for I have felt the same way since I was treated unfairly in a relationship. This is what I have come to find during years of research and growing up. You probably were not in a mutual relationship throughout the course of your relationship. I make that statement because being in a mutual relationship means that you have two people who are coexisting and doing what is good for the relationship. They are giving positive energy to the relationship and to one another. Many relationships today are one-sided relationships, which means that one of you is doing for the relationship and the other is doing for himself or herself. In many cases, the both of you are selfishly doing for yourself in an attempt to get whatever you can out of the relationship.

This type of relationship never works long term because it is selfish, dishonest, disloyal, greedy, and insensitive because it takes and steals vital loving nutrients that a relationship needs in order to survive. A relationship goes through its ups and downs, but if you feed it patience, kindness, love, understanding, and honesty, you will find that it can grow and stand the test of time.

When you make the decision to date only one race of men, you limit your options and something inside of you dies without your even recognizing it. A piece of you dies because you have allowed what one man did to you to taint an entire race of men. I want you to allow yourself to think about that for a moment—an entire race of men has been excluded from dating you. You have totally eliminated an entire race of men because of what one or two men did to you. I know that there is nothing quite like being hurt emotionally when you are the most vulnerable. You can find yourself making drastic changes in order to eliminate further emotional hurt, even if it means not dating a certain race of men anymore.

I do believe that you could be having a drastic reaction to what could have been your fault in the first place. I know there are guys who are jerks and who are only looking for their own self-gratification, but there are always signs that he was a jerk, which you may have missed. You have the ability to be emotionally hurt by every race of man on the planet. The reality is that men are men and we can all be jerks, but if you believe that gender is a factor, then you will be sadly mistaken.

I want to share another story with you concerning a relationship in which I was involved. I am by no means pawning myself off to be the best choice in a man, but I do know that my intentions and my heart are sincere when I approach a woman. There was a woman who was hired to work at my place of business. I saw her on a few occasions and said to myself how cute she was in appearance. She was a small-framed woman but seemed to be very athletic in her build.

I made up a lie and asked to see her in an office I was using. I know it wasn't professional to do this at work, but I wasn't going to miss out on this opportunity. Once she came into the office, I quickly told her that I lied and I apologized, but I really wanted to meet her and said that this was the best way to do it in private. She smiled and blushed once I said this to her, clearly realizing that it was a sweet gesture. I gave her the option to get to know me or for us to just continue to be coworkers. I stated to her that there was no pressure, but I had to at least ask because I was attracted to her. I later found out that by me saying that there was no pressure and we could just be coworkers, it made her choice so much easier.

Later that afternoon, she responded in a positive way and said that she wanted to get to know me. This story sounds romantic and dreamy, but be careful how something starts, for it may finish in a disastrous way. The first thing that I remember her telling me was that she had eight people inside of her. You heard me right— apparently, she had eight personalities inside of her, and I got a chance to meet all eight of those crazy-ass personalities. I thought she was joking when she told me she had eight personalities, but when a person tells you something like that, you'd better listen.

As the weeks went on, the number of people left inside of her went down. She would state that there were six left after a few weeks of dating. She would then say that there were only three left after a few more weeks of dating. I made the comment one day that she should inform me when there was only one left so I'd know who to address. I said that as a joke, but looking back, I have no idea what I was thinking of by placing myself in that situation. It was a bad decision, and I didn't use my common sense.

During that entire time of weeding out those eight personalities, I realized that she was interested in a relationship with a white man. You see, two black men to whom she was married had hurt her. When she looked at me, all she could see was the two men that hurt her emotionally and physically over the course of years. I soon realized after everything was over that she wasn't crazy. She was emotionally hurt from her past. Those scars remained, and I was only experiencing the aftermath of a woman who was hurting. She settled within her head that white men would treat her right, but she was absolutely wrong. What she really needed was the right man to treat her right, and it wouldn't matter what he looked like or his ethnic background.

You are probably wondering why she chose to be in a relationship with me if she really wanted to be with a white man. I believe that it was strictly for sexual reasons and a source of convenience. I was safe enough to have sex with, but she didn't feel safe enough to be in a real relationship with me at the time. I am a black man, and to her a black man causes pain, hurt, and emotional scars that are hard to heal. The physical action of sex didn't cause her pain or hurt; it just made her feel wanted for that moment. There are times when a woman's hurts can change her course and direction when it comes to her selection in men. One man can make a woman look at an entire race of men as all being the same.

The reason I knew that she was not feeling me was when we were at a Starbuck's having coffee and chai tea. I was having what I thought was a nice and mutual conversation with her at a small table. I noticed that a couple sat down behind me, but I never actually saw the couple. However, I felt their presence and noticed that she watched them the entire time. As we were in a conversation, I realized that she was fixated on the couple behind me.

I wanted to turn around to see what she was looking at, but it would have been obvious if I did. I decided to excuse myself and go to the restroom; this would give me an opportunity to take a peek at whomever she was more interested in than she was in talking with me. I got up and turned naturally to look behind me and realized that she had been staring at this interracial couple. In that short walk to the restroom, I wondered why she had a nice guy who genuinely loved her sitting in front of her face and she couldn't even see me. All she could see was a picture of this white man she has been dreaming about for so long.

I learned firsthand that the moments that affect your life can be the very moments that steal from your future. There is no guarantee that if she weren't so broken by her past that we would have lived happily ever after, but I would speculate that she will miss opportunities to be loved by someone who is genuine rather than by someone who is white.

THE DANGERS OF COMPROMISE

I found over the years that there are a few things in common that some men share when it comes to dealing with a woman. Men will sometimes watch and see what a woman will allow or compromise. If a man likes to spend time with the fellas, he will slowly integrate this into your relationship and watch how it is received by you. If your man was a flirt when you met him, he may try to continue that pattern even though he belongs to you exclusively, just to see how much flirting you will allow before it's too much. Deeper forms of compromise exist, and we need to cover them quickly. If you give up your goodies on the first date, he will definitely sleep with you, but you will not like the category he then places you in. Some men can be opportunists when it comes to women they are interested in.

I had a friend who was interested in a woman who had been abused in a prior relationship. She was living in a church refuge house as she recovered emotionally from her abuse. She was very attractive and just kept to herself, trying to get her life together. This so-called friend befriended her and they became close. As she felt more comfortable with him and told him about her past relationship problems, he slowly became her boyfriend. She believed in no sex before marriage because she wanted to do things differently from her past relationships. He said he respected that, but he started with respect and then worked her on the sex. Her need for sexual contact eventually overrode the promise to herself, and she slept with him. That was the first mistake and first signal that he wasn't the guy.

If your need is strong enough, you will do things you said you would never do. During an argument, he brought up the fact that she was supposed to be a Christian yet she slept with him outside of marriage. He actually threw that back in her face, but she didn't leave him. It is very important to establish right now what you will allow and compromise before you get to that point. She became damaged goods because she allowed her standards to be compromised by an infiltrator. He actually belonged in the acquaintance category, and there he should have stayed. But in her defense, he was fine and she was horny, so things happen in the real world of life, but I'm sure you know that already. Hopefully you will listen to the only thing that is always right: your common sense.

Some people will say that placing men in a category sounds silly. Let me tell you this: if enough men—or women, for that matter—have hurt you, you will see the importance of placing people where they belong as far as a relationship with you. If your girlfriend sleeps with your man behind your back, you will be hurt because she was your friend—and how could a friend do that to you? First of all, that is not the definition of a friend. You have to be careful whom you call a friend. We use the term "friend" too loosely in this generation.

If you place men in the right category, you can expect them to do certain things based on where you placed them. Do you want to understand men? If you answered yes, then I can tell you that that is an impossible task so stop trying to do it.

I have been a part of locker room conversations with men, and the conversations and topics are capable of making your head spin as a woman, but that is typical talk for a man. The conversations would make you laugh, cry, and realize that some men have no clue as to what a woman wants. The heart-to-heart discussions that men have one-on-one with each other are real talk, not the talk a man gives a woman when she asks him to communicate. This is spontaneous talk that may not be shared with a spouse or girlfriend for various reasons, but this is the type of talk that needs to be heard by women in order to understand their men.

It is a sad day when you see women giving up on men as a whole. It is even more heartbreaking when you see men give up on women as a whole. There are women who have been hurt physically, emotionally, and psychologically by a man, and they judge the entire male population based on *one* man's stupid actions. You do not need a book to tell you that you might be making bad decisions—just look back at your past relationships and you might see them. We tend to ignore the truth when we are chasing the euphoric desires of romance, but we don't see the reality of the relationship because we think we're in love and dismiss the warning signs. Consider this old saying: "If I only knew back then what I know now, things would be better." That is a bunch of bull, for you would still make the same mistakes with men even back then. Remember: these are the same mistakes you are making right now, even with all the knowledge you have attained.

You must never forget that change does not come easy for any human, so why would you think that you have cornered the market on changing men? Do you enjoy the challenge of trying to turn a frog into a prince? You can't manipulate a man in order to get the man you want. He is not a G.I. Joe action figure or a piece of clay that molds into this perfect man. The first rule should be to leave your ego at the door of the mind-set that you can change a man anytime you want to change him. If a man feels as if you are trying to change him before he is ready, he will slowly back away from you. He is backing away because "common sense" tells him that you are working your plan on him. What plan? The plan of turning this man into a husband against his will. Do not jump the gun and start talking marriage on the first date.

A few years ago, I took a woman to dinner at a Chinese restaurant that cooks the food at your table. We had an awesome conversation sitting at a table with strangers. We shared great stories about our childhoods and laughed the night away. We left and headed back to my apartment so she could pick up her car. I invited her in for a moment while I freshened up a little bit. She asked me if she could use my computer. The next thing I knew, she was on my computer searching a wedding dress website. She said, "This is the dress I will wear when you marry me!" What the hell! This was our first date and she was talking about marriage. If there is one thing women need to know about certain men, it's that marriage talk on the first date is bad etiquette.

Something inside of me immediately shut down, and I was in retraction mode. I slowly withdrew from her, and she had no understanding of why. Common sense tells you to just enjoy the evening so why bring up marriage? If a man is feeling you, he will change all by his lonesome. You will not have to ask him to change, for he will already be making the right adjustments. If a man wants to marry you, he will ask you. Just enjoy the moment and pump your brakes when you think that he is the one.

A man has learned how to treat women, whether good, bad, or indifferently, from the time he entered this world. You will never totally understand men, so you should start understanding that what you allow men to do impacts you in a positive or negative way. You don't need to understand men—just understand what you will and will not accept from a man. What is more important is that you understand your decision-making process and how you go about choosing a man and placing him in your personal category. Truth be told, it is less about your understanding men and more about your chronic bad decisions when it comes to choosing the right man to share your life. Men seek mates, but a woman chooses a mate, so choose wisely.

The best advice I could give is to never try to think like a man as some books have suggested. The idea of trying to think like a man insinuates that the man always has some trickery, games, and schemes going on that you have to figure out. There is no need wasting your time trying to think like that when some of the men you are trying to think like aren't good for you. If you find that you have to become a man mentally, when will you have time to be a woman naturally? Instead, know what you want and learn what your man wants from you and from a relationship with you. If you must know anything, know yourself first!

Allow yourself to just be a woman and allow a man to show you who he is through your exposure of him. There is good and bad in all of us, so take the time to learn both. All men are different, which makes understanding men that much harder. I would never ask a man to think like a woman, because to a man, that just doesn't make any sense. He would never understand the mind of a woman, but he would typically take the time to understand the woman he is with currently. To be honest, some women do not understand women, so how would a man understand the mind of a woman?

Men and women are confusing creatures when you get to the nucleus of how we think. We think completely differently to come to the same conclusion or opposite conclusions. We are both creatures of habit. We both lie to each other at some point in a relationship to avoid the truth about something. You can call it a white lie, black lie, or small lie. A lie is what it is ... a lie. We all have the ability to cheat on our mates, and some already do with precision. We all hear the same thing differently, and we can all judge one another based on a rumor or on past experiences, good or bad. So to say that you want to understand men is a tall feat, but like a woman, if you listen to your man, he will tell you what he needs as well.

CHAPTER 12

A GOOD MAN IS NOT HARD TO FIND

A good man is not hard to find, he just doesn't look like the guy you expected … that's all. What would happen if the man of your dreams didn't look the way you envisioned him? What would happen if he wasn't tall, athletic, and handsome with a six pack for abdominals? Would you still want him if he was just a regular guy who was short, not very athletic and had average or below average features?

While reading a *Men's Health* magazine one day, I saw a picture of a guy who was in great shape. Based on the chiseled physique he possessed, it was apparent to me that he puts a lot of time into training. I would gather that he watches what he eats and doesn't eat French cheesecake like the two slices I had last night. His abdominals were of the eight-pack variety, and here I thought a six-pack was the goal, but someone added two more stomach muscles to make things that much harder for men.

The guy in the photo could be considered physically appealing to men who want a body like his and to women who want someone with a body like his. He had a five o'clock shadow, broad chest, well-defined shoulders, large biceps, a nice tan, and he was wearing small swim trunks in the photo shoot. I have a good friend who is the opposite of the young model I am describing. He is around five feet seven inches tall and slightly overweight. His abdominals don't show the cultivating of an eight-pack; he actually has a one pack, which translates into a big stomach. He walks for exercise but definitely is not a chiseled specimen like the model. I'm not sure I want to see him in small swim trunks—but maybe you might. He is clean-shaven and maintains good hygiene.

What I am describing may not appear attractive on the surface, but that has been the problem of people for centuries, looking at the wrong things. If you were to meet my friend, you would find him to be the most charming teddy bear you have ever met. I know that there are many women out there that have a picture in their heads of the perfect guy. You may want your man to be tall, athletic, and handsome with a flat stomach. You may require him to pick you up at your house on his white horse, but I believe you will miss out on a really good man, even if he picks you up with his white donkey. I tend to feel that movies and romance novels have taken away the reality of what it takes to meet a man who is what you need and not what you desire.

I am not trying to suggest that there is something wrong with dreaming of someone like this and reading romantic novels, but why don't we consider the real guy for a moment? This is a guy who makes you feel like a woman when he is around you. This is the guy who makes you feel sexy when you don't feel sexy. This is the guy who loves you unconditionally when you can't even love yourself under your own conditions. This is the guy who supports your dreams and goals and doesn't put you down for dreaming.

I want you to understand this point: this guy is not perfect, and he will make mistakes, and you two will argue, but he will fight for your love and never leave or forsake you. You want a guy who takes pride in his character, not a guy who is trying to look more beautiful than you in a mirror. This is a free country, and you have the right to seek what makes you happy, no matter how vain and materialistic it may sound to the average person. I just don't want you to be fooled by the things that don't matter in the end.

What if the man of your dreams doesn't quite look like the man in your dreams? You may just be missing out on a guy who has a beautiful heart and a great character just because he doesn't meet your qualifications physically. Would you dismiss him for the guy you think is the man of your dreams but whom you have no business being with? I think the "man of your dreams" image gets in the way of the actual man who needs to be in your life in most cases.

If you have a list of things that a man needs to be or have, then I am not totally disappointed with you. If you keep it in the right context, this type of thinking corresponds with the standards I was talking about. But the list must be attainable, reasonable, reachable, and not too long. If you wouldn't qualify to date yourself according to your own standards, then revise the standards. You must allow for some human factors to weigh in. You have to always remember that he is not a programmable robot. You must be able to attain or possess at least 98 percent of the things on your own list before you demand them of someone else. You can't ask of a man that which you do not have yourself. You also must allow for the human element because men are not perfect, so don't demand perfection in your mate, for he will disappoint you just as you will disappoint him.

Sometimes you may have to see a man for where he is going rather than where he is right now. That takes vision, which you may not have yet. But he must be a man of potential and not an opportunistic boy who will take advantage of his situation with you.

As I have said, this book is be a basic commonsense approach to trying to understand why you have chosen poorly when it comes to men. I must first condition you to place men in their appropriate place, which is your personal category. Do not allow yourself to lose your basic common sense when it comes to men. If you allow the foolish notion that he is fine or that you can somehow change him, then these categories will mean nothing because you will repeat the cycle.

They will be easy to remember because there are only four of them. Here are the categories, listed in commonsense form:

1. Not good for you
2. Acquaintance
3. Friend
4. Personal relationship

Bonus: Marriage is never a category but oftentimes turn into a goal, like losing weight. Pump your brakes and make sure he is the one for you. A protector and keeper of your heart will never hurt you intentionally and will always be mindful of his actions and their implications. If your man does not know what hurts you, how can he truly know how to love you?

Not Good for You

This is an easy category, but at the same time, it will be the hardest one to master. I am not sure why this one is hard for so many people, but if you are able to master this category, you will lose a lot of excess baggage. I want to say this first before I get into this easy but difficult category. Every man has some good in him, but a particular man's "best good" may fall at the bottom of your "want list."

If the man lives with his mother for reasons other than he is disabled or taking care of her, he has to go in the no-good category. Do not promote him up the ladder just because he is fine and handsome. There is too much headache and pain to be with a fine, handsome broke brotha with no ambition. What's cute now will irritate the hell out of you later. If he is healthy enough to go to the club where he met you, then he is healthy enough to get a job and move out of Mama's house. A no-good man is easy to spot and takes little common sense to figure out.

If a man asks you for money, he goes into the no-good category immediately. No man should ask a woman for money, especially when you are getting to know each other. That is a sign that more is to follow down the road. If a man does not have a car and needs you to drive him on your date, he goes into the no-good category. Your man needs his own car, with car payments that are paid on time. Do these examples seem basic and easy to understand? If they do, then you have the ability to spot a no-good man. But here is what normally happens: if the man is finer than fine, you will forsake all of the no-good qualities and take a chance on him because he is fine and meets your expectations of the dream guy. And this is why you will be heartbroken in the end, attempting to change a man who isn't ready to change. If a man is unable to do the basics and it has nothing to do with his generosity to another human, place him in the no-good category!

Let me qualify one thing here. A man in the no-good category can move up in the category list, but you need to be able to accept what you may have to deal with in the relationship. Do not promote the no-good man to a relationship and then complain that he never takes you out, doesn't treat you like a lady, and never does whatever else you are claiming that he never does. You brought it on yourself when you tried to promote him to the relationship category based on the wrong qualities. He has to earn a move up before you arbitrarily promote him based on looks, sex, your biological clock, or whatever shallow reason you want a relationship. Common sense is the only way to avoid unnecessary pain. You will find pain with any relationship. The unnecessary pain is what you have to avoid as much as possible. I may sound a little harsh in this area, but I want to make sure that you protect your heart from guys who don't even care about you.

The Inner Man

Can a person change? I believe that people can change only when they have a reason to change. Forced change never lasts and is not from the heart. So do not try to change him! If you change him, it will not last. But if he changes himself, he is doing it out of respect and consideration for you and himself. You can always persuade change by asking for what you need in a relationship, but then leave it there and allow him to grow up. When a man realizes the things he doesn't have, only then will he understand what he needs to become. That is what you want a man to do, but you can't do this for him!

The commonsense phrase of the day: do not bring unnecessary headache to yourself by trying to change someone who is not ready or capable of changing. Some men are just what they are in your life—not good for you! That is where they belong, and that is where some of them should stay. Remember: he has you in his own category as well. You may be the girl he can sleep with every now and then. However, common sense tells me that that is not what you want to be known as when it comes to men. We all want respect, but when we are in the middle of disrespect, sometimes we don't recognize it because we want love.

The no-good man is anyone who cannot bring anything to the table or brings trouble in many forms. A man who says that he is divorcing his wife but spends months making excuses and you see no divorce resulting is not good for you. A man who only shows affection when he wants sex is not good for you. A man who is verbally or physically abusive is not good for you. A man who is always unreachable at a time when you should be able to reach him is not good for you. Use your common sense and separate what you want versus what you need. A short-term relationship is not what you want right now. What you need is someone who will be a life partner. Stop compromising and start demanding more from yourself and more from men. If you've been with the right man, you should feel good about yourself at the end of the day.

I know that life can be cruel, but if the man has fallen on hard times, he is sincere with his intentions, he is trying to meet your needs, and he loves you, then he may be worth stepping out on a limb for. You will have to use your common sense in evaluating and deciding whether you are willing to allow a person like this to love you without it turning into a messy encounter. These will not be easy decisions, and that is why this is the easiest yet hardest thing because you never really know. Keep it simple and use common sense. What you wouldn't do to hurt yourself personally, don't allow a man to do to hurt you.

Identify and categorize the not-good-for-you people in your life. Without being nasty about it, let them know exactly where you stand with them. Make sure you are clear internally about your future dealings with them. Resist when they persist and be resolute within yourself that they stay in that category. Only pursue a closer interaction with them when you are ready—and not a moment sooner. Your persistence will be the deterrent to those who do not add to your life and a magnet to those who are worthy of your time.

I purposely didn't discuss acquaintances in depth, for I truly believe that you get them. You know little to nothing personal about them, but it is pleasant when you see them and exchange pleasantries with one another. They are not your friends, just people you know and see from time to time.

Friends are those you know personally. Friends always have your back at key moments, and they are dependable. They are not out to compete with you or hurt you in any way. Just remember that you probably should have a short list of friends. Not everyone is your friend, and you will normally find that out at a point when you really need someone and that person is gone.

Once you have eliminated the not-good-for-you people, you will start to enter the personal relationship. I'm not going to discuss this category, because we all handle our personal relationships differently. I will say that if you have truly understood the not good for you person, then you should see the good qualities in your personal relationship. No relationship is guaranteed; it's a trial by fire. You will have to be understanding and patient in order for a relationship to work. In order to be with someone for twenty years, you will have to get through the first twenty minutes of meeting that person. You will then have to get through the next twenty days of knowing him. It's important to realize that a relationship is a process, not a race.

Chapter 13

HOW MANY GIRLFRIENDS DO YOU HAVE?

This is not a particularly long chapter, but then again, it really doesn't have to be in order to make my point. It was early Monday morning, and I was headed to an appointment. While I was driving my daily forty-five minutes to my appointment, I was going back and forth between radio stations, trying to catch sports highlights on one channel and the day's top stories on the next channel. It was my normal routine when driving into work. I arrived a few minute early and proceeded to park in my favorite area. I popped my trunk and got out of my car. I had to get my jacket and notebook out before I could lock my car. After I retrieved my articles, closed the trunk, and hit my car alarm button, I walked toward the front entrance.

I noticed the calmness of the ocean because my appointment was on the waterfront in a pristine location overlooking the Atlantic Ocean. I noticed the boats on the water and the naval ships floating in the background. I am retired military, so the ships have always been an enjoyment to watch. Once inside the building, I headed for the elevator. After a brief elevator ride, I walked in the room and noticed three women already there. I said good morning and had a seat in one of the open chairs. I placed all my belongings on the floor beside me and sat down at the table to listen to the conversation.

A few minutes later, a woman walked into the office. She had a little boy with her that turned out to be her son. While the women marveled at how handsome he was, I sat back saying nothing while noticing how shy he was with responding to everyone's smiles and attempts at conversation. "How old are you, young man?" one of the women asked. The little boy mumbled, "I'm five years old," and he held up five fingers.

The next question that was asked had never taken me by surprise before, because I had heard the question on many occasions. I was just a kid myself when I first heard it asked of me. The difference was that for some strange reason, this time I had a completely different internal response to the question. The woman asked, "How many girlfriends do you have?" Without hesitation, the boy raised two fingers of his right hand. The group of adult women in the room gave a congratulatory gasp and collectively said, "Well, all right then!" This made it sound fine to have more than one girlfriend. I sat there marveling over what I was witnessing, but I never said a word in opposition. Instead, I noticed a flaw in how we approach little boys when it comes to girlfriends and treating women. The flaw was clear and vivid in that very moment, but I think I was the only person who noticed it. The women in the room seemed to have fun with his answer and gave him this twisted form of encouragement. I wondered if this would still be considered cute if this child of five years old was now a man of twenty-five or thirty-five years old. Would it be acceptable and cute to the women if they found themselves one of the two women he was dangling on the side?

Of all the types of questions that went through my mind, the real question that bothers me is that I wonder if, with the comments that are unconsciously made, we are preprogramming our boys to be the very thing we don't want in a man.

CHAPTER 14

THE WORD WRONG IS A METAPHOR

The real reason that you keep, and will continue to keep, attracting the wrong men in your life is simple: *you are a woman!*

I know that is not what you wanted to hear, but it's a true statement. You probably wanted to hear me say something more psychological than that, but I am being quite psychological in my assessment. Please allow me to explain what I mean when I say that you attract the wrong men because you are a woman. The term "wrong" is a metaphor for the choices you make, and it is an adjective as well.

Wrong: *not correct or accurate; holding an incorrect opinion about a person, thing, or matter; not the intended or desired one; not functioning correctly.* (This is a great explanation.)

In other words, he can only be the wrong man when you have determined that he is not the right man. You can only determine that a person is the wrong man when you spend quality time with the person. You will attract *all kinds* of men in the circles that you frequent and in circles that you pass through just because you are a woman.

You can be a doctor, lawyer, nurse, waitress, stripper, single mother, or a divorced woman; it doesn't make a difference. All kinds of men are in the circles that you frequent, and among them are the wrong men for you. It is up to you to discern between what you need and what you want, what is right and what is wrong. It is ultimately your decisions that are the problem, not the men. A wrong man looks the same as a good man until you spend quality time through conversation and observation. Then and only then will you see the differences, and your decision from that point on will determine your level of hurt or happiness.

You are God's creation, you were made in the image of God, and you were made to be attractive to men ... all men! You will attract every kind of man in your life during the weeding out process. You will attract the tall man, short man, fat man, skinny man, crazy man, slow man, obsessive man, lazy man, pimp man, player man, and scrub man. People like this come in different colors and from different financial backgrounds.

Have you ever tried to find a four-leaf clover among an eclectic array of grass in someone's yard before? Hard, isn't it? As kids, we would do this all the time, and let me tell you that it wasn't an easy task. You really had to focus and look for that unique four-leaf clover. Rarely would you find one, but on occasion it was possible even to find more than one. You had to look through the grass and use your hands to slowly move the blades of grass around to expose the clover's shortcomings of just having one leaf, two leaves, or none at all. In your search, you didn't pick up every clover, but at times you found yourself picking up one, only to find out that it had three leaves. It tricked you for a moment, but you learned to look harder next time. But in your persistence, you knew you were getting close.

Was it a painstaking task to find that four-leaf clover among all of those that weren't four-leaf clovers? Yes! Did it take some time, effort, and patience on your part? Yes! Was there a reward in the end? Yes, but that depends on the reward you were seeking. But it was teaching you a lesson that you did not even recognize. You will not find the perfect man locked away in some foreign village waiting for you to come with a key to unlock him and take him home. Finding the man for you takes some time, persistence, patience, and the proper decisions made on your part. Finding the right man for you takes self-development on your part. Finding the right man is not bringing old relationship baggage with you into the new relationship.

The first woman was made to be attractive, alluring, desirable, enticing to the eyes, and a helpmeet to her man.

Women were made to be funny, serious, strong, emotional, nurturing, motherly, sensitive, and forgiving. What man wouldn't be attracted to those qualities? The right man and the wrong man would be attracted to the exact same qualities. So what will set the right and wrong man apart? It will ultimately be the man that you decide to be the keeper and protector of your heart. Will you make the wrong decision? At times, you may, but you must not give up and throw the baby out with the bathwater. Don't give up on men just because of one man.

All men have an agenda when it comes to a woman. Some agendas are pure, with all good intentions. A man may just want you to notice him and want to get to know you, without any tricks, games, or gimmicks. However, other agendas are bad, with only selfish reasons as the nucleus of their origin. You know the type; he wants to get you in bed, wants to move in with you, or use your car. You must discern what agenda the man possesses for you, and you must do it as soon as possible. This is why there will always be heartbreak when it comes to love. The reality of knowing that a guy who was interested in you only wanted sex or something financial that had nothing to do with the real you is an eye-opener. So the reality is that you will always attract the wrong man until you find the right one.

You can sometimes find that unique four-leaf clover right away and run him off because you were not ready for him. Some women believe it is all the man's fault for the reason a relationship failed.

Reality check! You are as much to blame as he is to blame. But as we so often do, we make it sound as if the other person is the villain and portray ourselves as the victim. The truth is that sometimes both of you are the villain and victim at the same time.

By nature, the wrong man in your life is supposed to do what wrong men do, so why are you surprised when you've been done wrong? You're supposed to meet the wrong man; this is the process that allows you to meet the right man. All men are the wrong men until you get to know them. Remember: if he's not the man for you, don't get all bent out of shape when you meet what you thought was the right man. Do not force the wrong man to be your man until you find the right one. This is a bad decision that will leave you frustrated. Patience is a virtue, not your enemy!

You are probably wondering how long it will take to find the right man. The answer is that it will take as long as it takes. The problem is often not that you seem to attract the wrong men but you seem to have not taken the time to define what kind of man you need in your life. You can't ask a man to meet all of your needs while assuming you've met his needs just because you're a woman. We live in a microwave society, where we have to have everything right now. Relationships take time to develop and mature into something special and valuable.

As I am writing this, a friend of mine messaged me through Facebook to tell me she is divorcing. She just married back in August, and this is March. I felt she rushed into the relationship, but she told me, "I know what I'm doing." Truth be told, sometimes we have no idea what we are doing and what it is doing to us until it's too late.

In closing, take your time, slow down, and enjoy the journey. A man is out there for you, but you don't just want any man—you want the man who will become something special to you. You want a man who will really love you through sickness and health and not just recite it on your wedding day. You want a man who will support your dreams and goals. This man will not be perfect, and he will piss you off at times, but he is not supposed to be perfect. He is supposed to be a human with flaws but a human who knows how to love. You want a man that when you tell him you're pregnant, he will be overjoyed because he loves you and his new baby-to-be. That man will protect you and that baby and not try to act as if you two didn't make this baby together. You don't want a man to say, "So what are you going to do?" This is a man that cares only about himself and how you are inconveniencing him. I say all of that to say this: you want a man who places your well-being over his own. That is a man with staying power, the trait you should pursue. That is the essence of the right man!

Acknowledgments

I would like to say **THANK YOU** to some people who have poured kindness into my life in a tremendous way. I could never be able to say how I feel about all of you, so I hope this conveys in a small way what you have meant to my growth and to this project.

I want to thank Danielle Batiste for encouraging me to write this book. Her telling me that I need to publish this was the first time someone believed that this was possible. If it had not been for her and her example as a published author, this probably would have remained on my computer.

Thanks go to my mother, Vivian Johnson, for always being supportive of whomever I brought to meet her. She always allowed me to love whomever I wanted to love, without any negative comments. How she lived her life through tragic situations is something I will never forget, and that is why I work so hard in order to make her happy. I thank God for her, and I will continue to make her proud of me.

I want to thank my father, Carnel Jordan, for being someone who I know always wanted me with him, and I understand why that couldn't be at times. You may be my father, but I will always call you Dad.

I wish to send a special thanks to Ronald "R. J." Johnson. You were a blessing in my life, and although you are no longer with us, I will never forget what you brought to our family. You were more like my second father than a stepfather.

I want to thank AuthorHouse for giving me the opportunity to publish my book. Your patience and attention to detail was superior. Your staff is great and it showed in the final product!

I want to thank my sister Angela Johnson; my mentors Darnell and Traci Self; Bishop Nate and Valerie Holcomb; Pastor Charles and Rochelle Nieman, CSM (ret); Terry Porter, CSM (ret); Robert House, MSG (ret); Rita Reeves, SFC (ret); Anastacio Moncada, SSG (ret); Victor Molina, MSG; Kevin Haley, SSG (ret); Terrilyn Williams; Cleveland Gates; Dr. Larry Black; Tracey Rentas; and my brother Garrick Lamont Johnson. You all were supportive of me finishing this book and helping me when I was stuck on certain days in ways you may not have realized. You all are priceless! If I have missed anyone, please charge it to my head and not my heart.

I truly Love You All

About the Author

CURTIS JORDAN knew there was more to his life than what existed inside a poor community called Huntersville, where he grew up as a child. He lived with his grandparents, who always provided a stable environment for him as he was growing up.

He went on to join the army and traveled all over the world—to such places as Australia, South Korea, Japan, and the Fiji islands—and he lived in Hawaii for four years. During his travels, he experienced many cultures and different lifestyles that never existed in the small town of his youth.

In 1968, Curtis Jordan was born to Carnel and Vivian Jordan in Portsmouth, Virginia. He quickly realized that reading was a way that would either promote him or expose him. During a sixth-grade reading comprehension lecture, he realized how important reading was when a teacher wanted to place him at a reading level below his classmates because of his poor reading demonstration. That incident made him develop into an avid reader, which increased with intensity after he graduated high school and joined the

Army. He read comic books, the Bible, and other various books, and he took classes on speed-reading. Over the years, his love for reading developed into a love for writing. He realized that he was easily able to write short stories fluidly, and his friends wanted to read them.

Curtis had the opportunity to give some advice to a woman about a man she was dating, and that experience led him to put his thoughts about the outcome on paper. It was fifteen years later before he decided he had something that should be shared with women who may feel as if they are unable to find a good man. He understood that a woman's choice is crucial and that maybe it was more precious than most women had ever considered.

He found himself making subtle suggestions whenever his female friends asked for advice concerning men and relationships. His advice developed into a real concern for the kinds of men that he saw his friends choosing. This all became personal for him when someone very close to him made a bad choice in a man. The relationship ended with this person being heartbroken and left a single parent with a disabled child. This incident sparked Curtis into writing what has now become a book on the importance of choices.

Curtis is a retired army veteran with twenty years of military service, and he is a licensed respiratory therapist. His image is featured at the Bird Aviation Museum and Invention Center in Sagle, Idaho, for his work with transport ventilators while serving on the U.S. Army Burn Flight

Team. He holds an Associate degree in Network System Administration and a Bachelor's degree in Information System & Cybersecurity.

Curtis Jordan is single and the proud father of three sons, Curtis Jordan II, Dondre' Jordan, and Darien Jordan.